ZERBANOO GIFFORD

A senior journalist, Farida Master has been an author and editor with several publications for the last thirty years. She started off as a rookie journalist in a star-studded world and soon went on to edit magazines like *Stardust*, *Citadel* and *Society Fashion* – all from the Magna Group of Publications.

Invited to be the editor of the *Pune Times*, she was instrumental in turning the paper around and increasing its circulation. Her Monday morning feel-good column, 'Cheers Pune', with its large fan-following, contributed towards it.

Farida's fascination with success stories motivated her to continue writing for several publications even when she found a new perch in Auckland, the city of sails. She wrote for publications including *The Aucklander*, *Woman's Weekly*, *Herald on Sunday*, *The New Zealand Herald* and *Her Business*, apart from writing for publications overseas.

Currently, she is the news editor of the community paper *Botany and Ormiston Times* from the Times Group.

Though Farida authored *The Making of a Legend*, the life sketch of Dr K.B. Grant, she believes her incredible journey so far was to prepare her to take on the challenge of *An Uncensored Life*.

ZERBANOO GIFFORD

A senior journalist, Farida Master has been an author and editor with several publications for the last thirty years. She started off as a rookie journalist in a star-studded world and soon went on to edit magazines like *Stardust*, *Citadel* and *Society Fashion* – all from the Magna Group of Publications.

Invited to be the editor of the *Pune Times*, she was instrumental in turning the paper around and increasing its circulation. Her Monday morning feel-good column, 'Cheers Pune', with its large fan-following, contributed towards it.

Farida's fascination with success stories motivated her to continue writing for several publications even when she found a new perch in Auckland, the city of sails. She wrote for publications including *The Aucklander*, *Woman's Weekly*, *Herald on Sunday*, *The New Zealand Herald* and *Her Business*, apart from writing for publications overseas.

Currently, she is the news editor of the community paper *Botany and Ormiston Times* from the Times Group.

Though Farida authored *The Making of a Legend*, the life sketch of Dr K.B. Grant, she believes her incredible journey so far was to prepare her to take on the challenge of *An Uncensored Life*.

ZERBANOO GIFFORD

AN UNCENSORED LIFE

FARIDA MASTER

For Armaity & Nauroz

Thank you for you wonderful

work for the Community

Love Zerbanoo

HarperCollins *Publishers* India

First published in India in 2015 by
HarperCollins *Publishers* India

Copyright © Farida Master 2015
Photographs © Pradeep Shetty 2015

P-ISBN: 978-93-5177-636-9
E-ISBN: 978-93-5177-637-6

4 6 8 10 9 7 5 3

Farida Master asserts the moral right to be identified
as the author of this work.

The views and opinions expressed in this book
are the author's own and the facts are as reported by her,
and the publishers are not in any way liable for the same.

HarperCollins *Publishers*
A-75, Sector 57, Noida, Uttar Pradesh 201301, India
1 London Bridge Street, London, SE1 9GF, United Kingdom
Hazelton Lanes, 55 Avenue Road, Suite 2900, Toronto, Ontario M5R 3L2
and 1995 Markham Road, Scarborough, Ontario M1B 5M8, Canada
25 Ryde Road, Pymble, Sydney, NSW 2073, Australia
195 Broadway, New York, NY 10007, USA

Typeset in 12.5/16 Garamond by
R. Ajith Kumar

Printed and bound at
Thomson Press (India) Ltd.

To my daughter Sanaya and Zerbanoo's grandson William Makepeace for adding a beautiful dimension to the kaleidoscope of our lives and filling it up with clarity, love and light.

CONTENTS

PREFACE

There is a good reason why you are holding a copy of *An Uncensored Life*. A moment of truth has led you to it. A similar unknown force drew me to take up the project of penning the biography of the inimitable Zerbanoo Gifford.

A compelling desire to explore an extraordinary life drove me to drop everything I was doing, leave home, hearth and husband in New Zealand and zoom halfway across the world. I found myself in the Forest of Dean, an ancient woodland believed to be the inspiration behind J.R.R. Tolkien's mysterious woods of Middle Earth. This is where Zerbanoo now resides with her husband Richard.

Living with Zerbanoo was a mind-expanding experience that allowed me to explore the core of her very being. One of her friends had warned me at the onset of this mémoire:

Zerbanoo dares to say it the way it is – 'Uncensored'.

She is unafraid to break the rules when it comes to fighting for a just cause – those who know of Zerbanoo's vast reservoirs of inner strength have drawn comparisons to Xena, warrior princess. I was witness to the wrath of Zerbanoo when Sanaya, my daughter, was unjustly detained by the authorities at Heathrow Airport for almost eleven nightmarish hours.

As we were kept in the dark about the reason for the hold up, we hadn't a clue as to why a twenty-two-year-old with a legitimate New Zealand passport would be kept waiting endlessly.

Sanaya had travelled from New Zealand to India to spend time with her grandmother and planned to holiday in England before returning to New Zealand. On finding that all communication channels had been suspended, Zerbanoo contacted Mark Harper, Minister for Immigration, who also happened to be the Member of Parliament for her constituency, the Forest of Dean. She was immediately put through to his advisor at the Home Office. However, nobody could give her a plausible explanation when she demanded to know why Sanaya was being treated like a suspect immigrant.

Richard, Zerbanoo's husband, a consultant lawyer with the world-renowned law firm, Clifford Chance, had also made contact with the immigration department. He was steadily and painstakingly working through bureaucratic red tape. The eleven hours felt like eleven years. We were then horrified to hear that Sanaya was going to be put on a flight to India. What was worse, it was to be a night landing in Amritsar, a city that was wholly unknown to her.

We raced to the arrival lounge at Heathrow Airport's terminal three and were directed to a public phone and asked to hold on until someone decided to answer it. An aloof voice assured us endlessly that our call was important to them, while impatient passengers queued up behind us. Zerbanoo refused to hang up. Finally, after fifty-five minutes, an immigration official came on the line.

Although a part of me was silently screaming for help, another on autopilot observed the sheer power Zerbanoo exuded with her presence. In hindsight, I can see that there was a good reason for this whole fiasco. It was destiny demonstrating to me what Zerbanoo was capable of achieving for those in despair.

Despite being numb with worry about just how traumatized my daughter would be feeling embroiled as she was in this bureaucratic botch-up, I appreciated the way Zerbanoo's took control of the situation. Something about her gave me the confidence that if there was one person in the world who could stop an international flight from taking off, it was Zerbanoo Gifford.

The immigration officer promptly passed the buck onto another official who had left for the day, and refused to shoulder the responsibility of untangling the mess.

At this point, Zerbanoo decided to change tack and mutated into her true form. Not one for mincing words – she was uncensored! She dealt with the crisis in her signature style. She read the riot act to the immigration officer that unless he wanted to precipitate headlines about an international incident in the following day's newspapers, he should take the necessary steps to sort out the matter. She firmly told him he had the power to stop the unjust deportation of an innocent New Zealander with a sterling record. Something in her voice must have convinced the officer-in-charge that she meant business.

Just minutes before the plane was ready to take off, Sanaya was asked to disembark. Much as Sanaya was desperately hoping to hear those words, she couldn't believe her ears.

Zerbanoo was Sanaya's heroine. She represented an uncrushable spirit that preserves moral order and righteousness in a chaotic world.

In the village of Newnham on Severn where I was researching and writing this biography, Zerbanoo and I often went for evening walks by the River Severn. This river is the longest in England and famous for a curious phenomenon: during certain high tides, huge waves surge upstream against the river's current, thus breaking all norms of gravity and science. Zerbanoo is like the Severn. Also, like the river, she is giving and attracts the power abundance. This timeless river carries within its bosom the countless stories of the people on its banks. It travels far and wide, touching lives just as Zerbanoo does.

ONE

LIVING THE ADVENTURE

Wired differently, Zerbanoo's life theme reads as one of daring adventure; taking risks without letting the fear of consequences restrain her free spirit. Whilst most people would ask 'can I?' Zerbanoo dives head-first into the challenge saying, 'why not?' She springs into action even before finishing her sentence, leaving people speechless in her wake. Little wonder that Zerbanoo's life has, like lightning, followed an erratic route, difficult to predict and impossible to follow, yet cannot be ignored for the immense effect it has on everybody around.

Zerbanoo's mother, Kitty, now in her nineties, recalls one particular incident that captures the essence of her daughter's spirit even as a child. It was a hot and sultry evening in Calcutta, India, when Kitty made an attempt at disciplining her toddler for being naughty. She told Zerbanoo to stand facing the wall. It was a tried and tested method of disciplining children, and Kitty, who had been personally trained by the famous Italian child educationist Madame Montessori, was confident it would work.

When Zerbanoo was released from her sequestration, she stubbornly held her ground because, in her mind, she had been unfairly treated. Kitty retired to bed believing young Zerbanoo would soon tire of her obstinacy, abandon her self-imposed quarantine and go to bed.

The next morning, Kitty found her daughter in a soaking nappy, standing in the same position. Kitty couldn't believe her eyes or comprehend how, despite the Calcutta heat, the scowling toddler could continue maintaining her mute protest in the exact same way she had been the night before. Nothing Kitty said could persuade Zerbanoo to give in. It was only after she had apologized for punishing her, that an exhausted Zerbanoo agreed to go to bed.

Kitty wanted Zerbanoo to learn independence and have the best education available in England and so when she was eight she was sent to Godstowe School in High Wycombe, which is halfway between London and Oxford. It was a private boarding school known for its discipline and academic rigour. Enid Blyton's daughter, Gillian, also studied at Godstowe, which is probably why the school had been the inspiration for the setting of the famous Malory Towers series. The school inspired Zerbanoo differently.

Up until then, Zerbanoo had led a carefree life at the family hotel in Central London. She had the best of all worlds as she spent her long summer holidays in India with her grandmother and her cousins who adored her. Zerbanoo had never been separated from those she loved.

The English boarding school was a shock to her system. She felt alienated and homesick. It wasn't long before she, along with four of her young schoolmates, hatched an ingenious plan to run away. It was an escapade straight out of Enid Blyton's The Five Find-Outers.

Early in the morning on the appointed day, deftly eluding the stern eye of the housemistress, the girls crept out in their dressing gowns that camouflaged the day clothes they wore beneath it. As soon as they were past the imposing school gates, they followed the route they had charted from High Wycombe on the A40 highway all the way back to London.

The thought that Miss Webster, the headmistress, would discover their great escape within a few hours and report them to the police as missing, hadn't crossed their mind.

Zerbanoo and her intrepid mates were captured and brought back to school in a police car. Each of them was made to write out letters of apology both to the police and to their parents.

Fortunately, Miss Webster had a sense of humour. It saved Zerbanoo and the others from being rusticated.

An excerpt from the letter addressed to her parents read:

This morning at 6.30 your daughter and four others of the same age dressed themselves and left school. They wore afternoon dresses and went without coats but wore vests to keep themselves warm. In a laundry bag they carried toothbrushes, towels and face flannels, so apparently they didn't intend to forget personal hygiene. They had dressing gowns which they wore in case they were seen on the way out of school and left them by the kindergarten. They then set out for London to go to Caroline Campbell Salmon's home. As they realized the journey was a long one, they intended to earn some money on the way (presumably for food), but seemed to be vague about the kind of employment they

intended to obtain. I believe one idea was to earn money
by singing.

The letter ended on a positive note, saying:

Although it would not be a good idea for them to know it,
I think their sense of adventure is to be commended and I
feel sure that they had no idea of the anxiety and trouble they
would cause. However, I believe they were well aware that
they were being naughty.

Miss Webster's fair but firm assessment of the girls despite
their defiance of authority demonstrated that she was a fine
judge of character. Miss Webster was astute enough to know
that the worst punishment she could give Zerbanoo was to stop
her from seeing her parents in the six weeks that followed. The
tone of her letter indicates that perhaps she discerned a spark
in Zerbanoo which needed to be guided and nurtured.

Another incident that showcased Zerbanoo's fearlessness
and ability to think on her feet was recounted by her godmother,
Mappie Dhatigara, wife of Air Marshal Edul Dhatigara and
treasured friend of Zerbanoo's mother, Kitty. In the late eighties,
when they were travelling in a tourist bus in Kashmir:

Suddenly, our bus came to a screeching halt. We were taken
unawares as a group of men with guns jumped into the bus
and threatened us with dire consequences. Everyone froze
with fear given the tense situation in Kashmir at that time.
But Zerbanoo's mind was ticking fast. Keeping her cool, she
realized she had to act quickly to save the other passengers'

lives. Somehow she realized that the men were not prone to attacking women and children. She also surmised that they probably could not read. It was a now or never moment to intervene. Running from the back of the bus where she was sitting, Zerbanoo looked at the hooded men squarely and dramatically whisked her gold business card from her bag. Brandishing it in the air, she shouted confidently, 'Do you know who I am?' The masked men were taken aback. We were all wondering what Zerbanoo was up to. Thank God, her bluff worked. The terrorists looked quite puzzled as they passed the embossed card amongst themselves. I am still not quite sure what went through their minds but much to everyone's relief, they got off and waved the bus on. Zerbanoo's extraordinary courage saved the day and our lives. Some years later in an editorial in the *Times of India*, Bachi Karkaria labelled Zerbanoo as an AK 47 with red nail polish. Maybe the bandits instinctively realized that themselves and decided to let us go.

Zerbanoo's life is peppered with such stories – some courageous, some, downright outrageous.

In the late seventies, Zerbanoo was travelling with her father, Bailey, from India to England with a stopover in Egypt. The father and daughter who were travelling abroad for the first time together were keen to head for one of the seven wonders of the ancient world, the pyramids in Egypt. However, upon reaching Cairo airport they discovered that Zerbanoo did not have the required inoculation documents. There had been an epidemic in India at the time of her travel and the customs regulations required all passengers to have mandatory booster shots before setting foot on Egyptian soil.

Zerbanoo was neither aware of the epidemic nor the rules. When she got to the immigration desk, the officer asked for her inoculation papers and questioned her roughly about why she wished to visit Egypt. Without batting an eyelid, Zerbanoo quipped, 'I'm Queen Nefertiti of the Nile. I am here to see the pyramids in Luxor.'

Her flippant tone coupled with her brazen attitude landed Zerbanoo and her father in prison for three bitterly cold nights. It wasn't quite the holiday they were expecting.

Later, in an interview published in the British *Sunday Times* magazine, Zerbanoo admitted thinking the immigration official in Cairo needed to lighten up. Her father, grudgingly confessed that even in the discomfort of the prison cell, he was secretly impressed with the manner in which his eighteen-year-old, in the adjoining cell, induced the no-nonsense Egyptian prison officers into bringing her special vegetarian meals, not to mention an electric heater and extra blankets to keep her warm. At one point, Bailey wondered what the ruckus outside his prison cell was all about and then realized the gaolers were running from pillar to post to find English newspapers for his daughter, after Zerbanoo had regally informed them that, as she couldn't read Arabic, she would need English newspapers to pass her time. To Bailey, 'It seemed as if Zerbanoo had an innate gift of making difficult people feel good about themselves, as they fulfilled her every wish.'

TWO

HER FATHER'S DAUGHTER

Zerbanoo's ancestry can be traced back to a proud bloodline. At the beginning of the twentieth century, her maternal grandfather, Shapoor Mazda, along with a camel and three Iranian Zoroastrian friends for company, dared to negotiate the high dunes of shifting sands, and travelled from Iran to India. They trekked for four long years through the treacherous terrain of the Khyber Pass route. Mazda was only sixteen at the time.

The journey across borders in search of a better life proved to be a life-changing experience. His beloved camel didn't make it, but he did.

As soon as he reached the crowded shores of Bombay (now Mumbai), he made a living selling tea from his Persian samovar on the sidewalk to the poor people who were referred to as 'the untouchables' in India. Shapoor soon befriended them. It wasn't long before he became protective of his loyal clientele who started their hard, manual work very early each morning with only the warmth of his tea to fortify them. The higher caste Hindus objected to this and threatened the poor Harijans with violence. Shapoor, who had the strength and physical presence of a Persian wrestler, heard about the intimidation tactics. The Zoroastrians had suffered discrimination in Iran and he too had experienced the arrogance of those who used fear and bigotry against innocent people. Shapoor decided to befriend the Harijans and declared himself their champion. No one dared to threaten the workers again.

Shapoor's robust hardiness and business acumen paid off. From selling tea by the roadside, he started trading in other commodities. Like many young entrepreneurs, Shapoor needed equity to expand. In order to convince the moneylender, who lived below his bedsit, that he was a man of means, he sat up all night with his five silver coins and dropped them on the floor one after the other, over and over again. The tinkle of coins sounded to the man downstairs like he was counting his bags of money. The next morning, he approached his neighbour and explained that he required just a small loan for his new enterprise. The moneylender immediately agreed, saying it would be a privilege to invest in the trading venture of such a rich man. That is how Shapoor got his break.

Business flourished and he gradually earned goodwill and respect as a merchant of repute. Later he moved to Calcutta (now Kolkata), the capital city of the state of West Bengal in India, to further expand his business. Calcutta was, at the time, the centre of British rule in India and Shapoor knew his business would flourish there.

He was the first businessman to install large walk-in freezers and cold storage facilities for meats and other perishable products. Shapoor travelled every year to the United Kingdom to order the food and beverages. Just before the outbreak of the Second World War, he was astute enough to order the last container of Johnny Walker whisky from Scotland. He knew the British in India had a longstanding love affair with their whisky. They needed their tipple and were ready to pay for it. While he made a killing on the whisky, he also sold Ovaltine, a nutritious chocolate malt drink at cost price so that everyone could enjoy a good night's sleep.

Before long, by dint of hard work and great business acumen, he owned the equivalent of London's food emporium 'Fortnum and Mason's' in India. Shapoor Mazda was declared one of India's richest men and the title of Khan Bhadur was bestowed upon him. It was an acknowledgement of his extraordinary achievements, and philanthropy, which included the building of a girls' school in the town of his birth, Yazd in Iran. Having lost his only sister at a young age, he established the school in her memory. Shapoor felt that girls also needed to be educated and given life chances that were often denied to them. He was an early feminist believing that women, given the opportunities and a sound education, would soon catch up with men and outshine them.

Zerbanoo has the same default setting in her DNA template and possesses similar qualities.

Apart from her maternal grandfather's genes, Zerbanoo also inherited her maternal grandmother's genetic code, which was indelibly stamped with a desire for individuality that defied convention. Shapoor's wife, Jerbanoo, was a free spirit with an inexhaustible zest for life. A natural trailblazer, she thrived on living an unrestrained life of generosity and glamour. In the roaring twenties, she was one of the few Indian women to wear red lipstick and rouge. A devout fashionista, she cut a stunning figure draped elegantly in the finest French chiffon saris that she fastidiously colour coordinated with Italian shoes. Both, her daughter Kitty and her granddaughter Zerbanoo inherited her sense of style and élan.

Zerbanoo's feisty grandmother loved life as much as she loved horseracing. She thrived in an environment where the stakes were high. Every year, Jerbanoo travelled to London to take her son, nicknamed 'Daddy' by everyone, to his British boarding school. She then toured Europe, which included Monaco, to play roulette at the Place du Casino in Monte Carlo. Jerbanoo once witnessed a man sitting next to her losing his fortune at the tables. He had started the evening with a winning streak but then the tables had turned and he began to lose drastically. Something in him must have snapped and in desperation, he piled all his chips into the game and lost it all. He had a hunted look about him and he suddenly extracted a gun from his pocket and blew his brains out. As his blood splattered Jerbanoo's exquisite sari, the horror of the suicide seared itself into her brain.

On another occasion, at Folies Bergere, the world-famous cabaret music theatre for avant-garde shows in Paris, she happily suggested that her husband, Shapoor, use his binoculars to get his money's worth with a closer look at the scantily clad women in the show. There was no room for pretence or hypocrisy in her life, and this no-nonsense attitude was her legacy to her granddaughter.

Much as she loved life, Jerbanoo died suddenly. She was in her early forties when she bled to death overnight from a simple tooth extraction. Her mother's death came as a huge shock to Kitty who was barely a teenager then.

In those days, no one knew Jerbanoo had a bleeding complaint. This was an unfortunate facet of her genetic bequest to Zerbanoo. The grandmother and granddaughter also share the same name, with a difference only in the first letter. Jerbanoo was the Gujarati version of the Old Persian name, Zerbanoo, meaning 'Lady of gold'.

Jerbanoo wasn't the only one in the family with a zest for life. Her son-in-law, Bailey, was just as flamboyant.

Bailey's father, Rustom, Jerbanoo's elder brother, had died at an early age, leaving his young wife, Gover, a widow. Barely thirty-six, Gover was left to raise eight children on her own; four others had already died as babies. Bailey was the fifth and quick to grasp that, as a middle child, he was practically invisible in a noisy brood of attention-seeking children. He soon realized that the only person he could rely on was himself.

Although Rustom belonged to a wealthy Irani family settled in Poona, upon his death, his widow struggled to make ends meet. The difficulties only made Bailey stronger. They honed his survival instincts and strengthened his determination to make something of himself. Possessed of an adventurous streak, he loved to take chances.

Bailey established an ice factory in Bandra, Bombay. At the age of twenty-three, he was keen to tie the knot with his childhood sweetheart Katayun, nicknamed Kitty by the nuns at Loreto Convent School in Calcutta. Kitty was the second daughter of Jerbanoo and Khan Bhadur Shapoor Mazda.

The Indian summer of 1950 saw the newly married couple become parents of an energetic, bright-eyed baby girl. They named her Zerbanoo.

Years later, in an interview with the *Sunday Times*, Bailey

shared an intimate secret. He said he had felt his mother-in-
law's presence in his bedroom the night their first child was
conceived. He knew that Kitty would have a girl and that she
would be like her large-hearted grandmother, Jerbanoo.

Bailey was an extrovert determined to create a better life
for himself and his family. Following India's declaration of
Independence in 1947, he found himself toying with the idea
of breaking free from his business in Bombay and moving on.
The increasing price wars on ice and the absence of regulations
in business, made it difficult to make any profit. In 1950, Bailey
was resolved to move to London where his elder brother,
Gussie, lived.

Gussie, a genius in mathematics, had travelled to England
before the Second World War to study at University College
London. He was head-hunted by the Indian Civil Service
and would have had an amazing career under the Viceroy. He
never returned to live in India, having fallen in love with Vera,
an English girl, who wanted to stay in England. Instead, his
two younger brothers Fred and Buck joined him in England.
Together, they had started the famous Three Eyes coffee bar
in Soho, London. They took pride in the fact that the Calcutta-
born pop singer, Cliff Richard, had performed there. Tommy
Steele, the British Elvis, also got his first break at Three Eyes.

Bailey, in the meantime, was eager to take the plunge and
travel to England to join his brothers. Kitty was naturally
cautious about the unknown. Cradling her precious baby in her
arms, she did not want to make the long voyage to a new home.

Zerbanoo was only nine months old and it was too soon for
me to travel to England. My mother-in-law was really sweet

and she offered to help. She promised to look after Zerbanoo until we found our feet in England. Although it broke my heart to leave my baby behind, I knew Bailey's mother would take good care of her.

The first few impressionable years of Zerbanoo's life were spent in the warm embrace of her grandmother, whom she fondly called Bapai. Gentle and sweet-tempered, Bapai doted on her granddaughter and greatly influenced her formative years. Although Zerbanoo gives credit to the entire family of cousins, aunts and uncles saying, 'All of them had a stake in my upbringing,' she absolutely adored Bapai.

The foreword of the first book Zerbanoo authored gives a glimpse of the special relationship she shared with her paternal grandmother. The touching tribute of the *Golden Thread: Asian Experiences of Post-Raj Britain* was dedicated to Bapai. It read, 'Gover Rustom Irani, 1901-1984, out of love for her and because she symbolizes all that is best in Asian womanhood: selflessness, wisdom and beauty.'

Seeing Zerbanoo happily settled in her grandmother's arms, Kitty reluctantly agreed to accompany her headstrong husband to England. They boarded a ship embarking on what was soon to be one of the most physically and emotionally challenging experiences of Kitty's life. The rolling of the ship made her violently sick. Her world was literally tossing and turning.

The long haul and the choppy seas took their toll on Kitty. She felt abandoned and alone. Bailey was the life and soul of the party, having a rollicking time drinking with his new buddies on board, whilst she suffered silently in her cabin. He could hold his own wherever he went, even on the high seas, amidst hundreds of strangers aboard a weather-beaten ship.

As his son, Rustom, wrote years later in a tribute to his father: 'No one who met him forgot him. He was genuinely charismatic, with an infamous sense of humour. But, he had so many parts to his character. He was loud, yet reflective and sometimes very gentle; stubborn, yet conciliatory.'

Kitty reflects on their early days in a foggy London that seemed to be perpetually enveloped in a grey haze. This was soon after the Second World War.

We bought a magnificent old building near Hyde Park. The building had been the Jewish Club and home to many Jews escaping the Nazis throughout Europe. Our business plan was to convert the old, grim-looking building into a cheerful guest accommodation that we would call 'Heritage Hotel'.

The first thing we did towards achieving our vision was to freshen up the Victorian building with a new coat of paint. We started with the windows that had been painted black and then added beautiful curtains to make it look warm and upbeat. Bailey loved the hotel business.

In sharp contrast, Kitty was trying hard to cope with the workload. A complete stranger to domestic duties, she took the initiative to join a cooking class, learning the most basic skills such as how to boil an egg. She also enrolled in a class to learn the basics of housekeeping.

Kitty studiously took notes as the teacher gave detailed instructions on the finer nuances of dusting. 'Begin from the ceiling and gradually move downwards, towards the floor,' was how young ladies were initiated into the technique of dusting. Kitty also enrolled for sewing classes so that she could stitch curtains and cushions for the hotel, to save money. She learnt wallpapering and upholstery. With every new skill she acquired the business grew more profitable.

In the meanwhile, Bailey's elder brother, Gussie, who often travelled to India on business, accompanied an eager and bubbly Zerbanoo back to England. She was all of four, and it was the first time she had seen her parents since they left for London. Zerbanoo excitedly ran up and down the hotel stairs in what was to be her new home. The first thing she wanted to know was why the hotel was not coloured red, like the one in the Monopoly game she had played with her cousins in India.

Living in the family hotel suited her friendly extrovert temperament. Zerbanoo loved people and had a natural flair for playing hotel manager. She collected rent from the permanent guests living on the top floor as she chatted away nineteen-to-the-dozen with the hotel clients. Dealing with celebrity guests was a part and parcel of growing up in the hotel. A resident American lady named Polly Burnaby who had no family to call her own, was a particular favourite. Over the years, Polly became part of the Irani family and helped Kitty with looking after all her children ... Genie, Rustom and Naswan who had followed Zerbanoo after a gap of nine years. Polly taught Zerbanoo to read English. Up until then she was more accustomed to talking in Gujarati with her grandmother in Pune. Every morning, Zerbanoo ran to Polly's bedroom to wake her up so that they could play and read together. Years later, Polly died at

Zerbanoo's home where she had been staying, after a chronic illness. Her photograph still adorns Zerbanoo's office.

One of Polly's favourite stories was about the seven-year-old Zerbanoo who chirpily answered the hotel phone. Without bothering to make a note of the call or even verbally communicating the telephone conversation to any of the grownups at the hotel, she took the booking of a school group from Derbyshire.

Come Easter, a busload of thirty-six children accompanied by their headmaster drew up outside the Heritage Hotel. Bailey was flabbergasted upon seeing the big contingent arrive unannounced. When he questioned Mr Woods, the headmaster, about who had taken the reservation, he was told the voice on the phone had sounded like a young person's. Fortunately, the situation was salvaged as there were enough vacant rooms to accommodate the group. The school expedition to London returned every year for their Easter break and Zerbanoo continued to join the students on their London bus tour as their self-appointed sight-seeing guide until the hotel was sold upon Bailey's death.

Bailey taught all his children how to work every aspect of the hotel business. They had hands-on training in reception duties, welcoming guests, making beds, polishing furniture, cleaning toilets and showers and ironing linen. Bailey also showed his trainees how to shop at cash-and-carry stores, cook and serve breakfast and everything else required for running a successful hotel.

None of the training was wasted. Bailey taught Zerbanoo the skills for navigating different worlds. Her friends joke that she would make an excellent hotel inspector or auditor in the hospitality industry with the skills and eye for perfection she acquired while working for her father. Her early experience at the hotel would teach her to synthesize her business school education with street smartness, laying the foundation for her life's work. In her own words:

> I learnt everything they do not teach at the Harvard Business School from my father. Daddy taught me the dignity of work and that everything you learn in life is eventually useful. Now at the ASHA Centre I take pride in teaching volunteers how to make beds and be good housekeepers; and, most important, to serve with a smile.

Bailey mainly moved to England to educate his children to the highest standard. He enrolled Zerbanoo in one of the most exclusive girls' schools, Roedean, nestled in the seaside town of Brighton, to give her the best education money could buy. Nine years later, his younger daughter Genie was also enrolled at Roedean and then at the Swiss Institute, Le Rosey, near Geneva.

His sons Rustom and Naswan studied at Rugby School, one of England's oldest and most prestigious public schools, which was also the setting for Thomas Hughes's semi-autobiographical masterpiece *Tom Brown's School Days*. The invention of 'Rugby' is credited to schoolboy William Webb Ellis who broke the existing rules of a football match played in 1823 at Rugby School, to create the new sport.

Zerbanoo recalls:

In spite of sending me to one of the best schools in the world, my father never looked at my school report. He'd say with a twinkle in his eye, 'Now I need to de-educate you from all that education.' When driving me to school, Daddy would call Roedean *Wuthering Heights*. He had this thing about the book's characters Heathcliff and Cathy and their semi-savage love. A kind of passion that makes people feel alive and is a bit disturbing and out of control. Laurence Olivier, who played Heathcliff, lived very close to Roedean on the Brighton seafront, which we passed as we drove to school. The other connection to the *Wuthering Heights* characters was through my mother, who knew Merle Oberon, the famous Anglo-Indian actress renowned for her portrayal of Cathy. She had been my grandfather's secretary in Calcutta before becoming a Hollywood icon.

I used to call school 'Colditz', after the castle where the Allied prisoners of war were imprisoned by the Nazis. It looked so bleak and I knew there was no escaping from it. Looking back on those trips to school ... Daddy got a kick out of his old, rather worse for wear Ford which he insisted 'went like a bomb'. There would be plenty of parents arriving at school in their fancy Rolls Royces and Bentleys. I used to be slightly embarrassed and ask him to drive out fast. To which he'd give me a wicked smile and say, 'Now, now, no snobbery here, you're lucky that you haven't had to take a bus and walk up the drive to school.' He definitely made sure I was never out of touch with everyday life.

Bailey was large-hearted and always the first to raise his hand when it came to fundraising for charities. At the age of seventy-two, he enthusiastically took off with a group of youngsters to climb Ben Nevis, Britain's highest range with spectacular views of Scotland. He was the oldest in the group. Nevertheless, that didn't deter him from taking on the challenge to scale the lofty height of 4,409 feet to collect money for the mentally challenged. He was the youngest president of the City of London Lions Club and a Freemason. Zerbanoo has effortlessly taken on his mantle with her enormous fundraising drives for innumerable international charities.

Bailey didn't believe in spending money on himself. He was very thrifty and used his ingenuity to get the best bargains available. He would shop late at night, when perishable goods were being priced down, so as to get food cheaply. He would sweet-talk travel agents into informing him about last-minute distress sales on package holidays. It didn't take him more than an hour to pack his bags and jump on to the last available seat on the coach, so long as it was at a giveaway price. By the time he was in his seventies, he realized that the airlines had a list of people called 'Speed birds' who would fly to distant lands to personally deliver parcels to clients of the airlines. Bailey would charm the girls at British Airways and soon became their favourite speed bird and they would allow him to choose the places he'd like to visit. Thus Bailey travelled to every country on his wish list.

As soon as he had delivered the packages to the country of his choice, Bailey would book himself on a bus to further explore the cities. He was perpetually on a shoestring budget and stubbornly refused to spend his hard-earned money on expensive hotel rooms. He roughed it out, boarding the night train that would drop him to the destination of his choice in the early hours of morning. He was content with doing all his sightseeing during the daytime and spending the night travelling by train. Sometimes it meant spending the night at a bus shelter, but that didn't bother the man who believed 'A penny saved is a penny earned'.

Bailey's wanderlust had him sending postcards to Zerbanoo from exotic and unheard of places. One postcard that Zerbanoo received in the early sixties, when she first went to Roedean School, caused quite a stir as it was only signed, 'From Russia with love, 007'.

Zerbanoo's husband, Richard, describes his late father-in-law as, 'Quite a character, functioning beyond the bounds of logic. He would find inspiration in everything.'

Bailey gambled with the stock market and with life, making the most of every opportunity. Never shy of learning new skills, he learnt boxing at twenty, horse-riding at thirty, flew a plane at forty, learned bullfighting at fifty and skiing at sixty. He continued paragliding and skiing until he was seventy.

Bailey had an irrepressible sense of humour that endeared him to everyone. When expounding on his exploits in a Spanish bullring, he declared to everyone's amusement: 'I may be an amateur bullfighter but I am a professional bull-shitter.'

Zerbanoo recalls that however tired or tipsy her father was, he would never go to bed without saying his prayers. Bailey was a devout Zoroastrain. Zerbanoo says, 'He prayed every morning and evening without fail, doing his kusti, tying the sacred thread around his waist whilst paying his respects to the supreme creator, Ahura Mazda.'

Zerbanoo's brother, Rustom, reminisces, 'Bailey's religion was ingrained in his soul. Apart from his personal faith, he had a grand vision that the Zoroastrian global community would be represented by a worldwide body.'

His legacy was the World Zoroastrian Organisation (WZO), of which he was the founder president. He recognized the significance of the diaspora from Iran and India to the Middle East and Europe, Africa, Australia, New Zealand, Singapore, the USA and Canada, and realized that a worldwide body, even if partly symbolic, could help protect their heritage and rights. He campaigned for the WZO, usually alone, at his own expense, lobbying organizations such as the United Nations.

Rustom would be asked to tag along with Bailey for meetings at the UN and asked to wait in the foyer. After he had briefed the officials, Bailey would allude to his delegation waiting down in the reception area, hoping that no one would bother to check. The one time they did, Rustom had to hurriedly explain that the delegation was out for lunch and would be back soon, before making himself scarce.

Gradually, as the different facets of Bailey's character emerged, it became obvious that Zerbanoo is her father's daughter. Both are proud Zoroastrians, and quintessentially 'Type A' personalities. Like her father, Zerbanoo believes in immediate action, is energetic and passionately opinionated. It was hardly surprising that, although they saw eye-to-eye in most situations, they also had some heated arguments.

It was Bailey's quick temper that Zerbanoo found difficult to contend with all through her growing years. Like most men of his time, Bailey was a stereotypical alpha male and the patriarch of the family. He expected everyone at home to unquestioningly obey his every command.

Zerbanoo was equally strong-willed when she felt she was

justified in her stance. There was an instance when Zerbanoo, furious after a showdown with Bailey, walked out of the house. She was sixteen then. Adamant about not returning home, she spent a year at her uncle Gussie's house with her cousin Diane whom she adored.

Despite their differences, there was no denying that Bailey and Zerbanoo cared for each other deeply. When Bailey was diagnosed with terminal pancreatic and liver cancer in the winter of his life, it was hard for him to accept it. For someone who had such a zest for life, it was difficult to come to terms with death hovering in the wings. For Zerbanoo it was an opportunity to spend precious time with her father.

Even when he was seriously ill, he enjoyed doing the rock and roll with Zerbanoo, which he had taught her. She says, 'Daddy loved to sing and dance. His last words to me when he was dying were: "The show must go on."'

He was referring to a prior commitment that Zerbanoo had made, where she was to give a guest of honour speech at a new academy school in West London. However, reluctant to leave his bedside, Zerbanoo told her father she could easily cry off the appointment and the school would understand. Nevertheless, Bailey insisted she went, saying, 'No daughter of mine will ever let anyone down.'

Zerbanoo made him promise he'd hang in there until she returned.

She remembers rushing back from the public event to the ward at St. Mary's hospital in Paddington. She was by his bedside, holding his hand and encouraging him to make his journey onwards with the knowledge that he had lived a truly rich life.

Daddy was a fearless and a generous man who had given away all his wealth before dying. But he was worried about leaving us. I told him that he had led a good life and it was time to meet not only his maker but also his mother and his siblings who were waiting to welcome him home. I knew the end was near.

Mappie, my godmother, had flown in from India and had been driven straight from Heathrow to the hospital. I asked her to start our powerful Zoroastrian prayers as I held Daddy in my arms and kissed him goodbye.

In a touching tribute to her father some years later, Zerbanoo donated more than 4000 Old English rose plants to the ASHA Centre, which she had founded in Gloucestershire to empower the young to live life to the full as her father had done. The rose garden was created in memory of her father's love of roses.

Daddy loved singing the seventies' song '*I never promised you a rose garden*'. I thought what better way to remember him than to lay out a rose garden so everyone could enjoy it. He always wore a rosebud in his lapel and gave Mummy a dozen red roses for every wedding anniversary. He was an old romantic and I know that even now he is in the rose garden enjoying the fragrance and sheer splendour of the blooms. I think of Daddy whenever I see the roses, and when there is a rainbow in the sky I know he is smiling at me. I used to hate the rain because it would spoil my hair and make it frizzy, but he would always say, 'If you want to see a rainbow, you gotta put up with the rain.'

At the opening of the ASHA Centre rose garden in 2008, Zerbanoo invited the Zoroastrian community for the occasion. It was raining heavily, but then suddenly, as she was chatting with Glyn Ford, the guest of honour and European Member of Parliament for the area, the sun came out. Zerbanoo told all present that if her father was watching them and was happy, he would send a rainbow as a sign.

Later, as the buses full of Zoroastrians merrily left the gates of the ASHA Centre, Glyn telephoned Zerbanoo to announce that there was not just one but two brilliant rainbows over the River Severn.

THREE

TURNING POINT

Touring America in a Greyhound bus, on holiday with her mother, Aunty Mappie and her paternal grandmother Gover, whom she called 'Bapai', a curly-haired, wide-eyed, six-year-old, soaked in the vast landscape. She snuggled up to her grandmother.

Gover's own life journey had been an arduous one. As a child, she'd left Iran with her family, and arrived in India as a refugee. They had barely touched the Indian shores when her father passed away. Without knowing a word of the local language Gujarati, or English for that matter, Gover's mother had to learn to survive in a foreign land with four young daughters and a son.

Gover, the prettiest of the sisters, was married off at the tender age of fourteen to Rustom, a lad from a well-to-do Irani family in Poona. Gover went on to bear twelve children in quick succession before tragedy struck and she was left widowed in her early thirties.

She would often tell Zerbanoo how fortunate she was to be living in a modern world where she could educate herself and lead a fulfilling life. Modern women had options which had been denied to her generation. The bond between Zerbanoo and her grandmother was special. Bapai was always full of wisdom about how people should behave when faced with adversity. Zerbanoo instinctively felt reassured in her presence.

The bus ride through the southern states of America was long and tedious. Like her mother, Kitty, Zerbanoo was a bad traveller and was dreadfully sick throughout the journey. Her grandmother tried to distract her by chanting Zoroastrian prayers offered to Ahura Mazda, the God of light and wisdom. Zoroastrianism is a faith that proclaims the victory of good over evil.

Bapai was preparing Zerbanoo for her Navjote, an initiation ceremony not unlike the Jewish Bar Mitzvah, which would officially enfold and welcome her into the Zoroastrian faith. She told Zerbanoo that the prayers were conversations with God.

As the Greyhound bus stopped en route at stations, Zerbanoo observed that the black people who came aboard were treated differently. They always sat at the back of the bus. Even when they got off, they used different toilets, water fountains and restaurants. Everything was clearly labelled. This was before the Equal Rights movement for the blacks in America had started to make an impact on people's lives.

Zerbanoo was visibly upset. She instinctively felt that what was happening was wrong, and demanded to use the same facilities as the black people. Mappie, her godmother who was also on this trip, feels it was this experience of seeing blatant racial discrimination that played a role in shaping Zerbanoo's desire to champion the disfranchised.

Although Zerbanoo's family migrated to Britain in the early fifties with its rigidly class-ridden society, they never stopped their daughter from interacting with those who were classified as the 'Working class'. She happily befriended everyone.

Kitty fondly recollects how, as a young girl, Zerbanoo looked forward to the dustmen's regular visit to their family hotel.

She used to eagerly wait for them to turn up every week, promptly running into their arms the minute they arrived. It was the highlight of her week. They would play with her and throw her up in the air. She would always sing their favourite song for them: '*My old man is a dustman, he wears a dustman's cap, and he wears cor blimey trousers and lives in the council flat.*'

Years later, when engaged in politics, Zerbanoo took great interest in public refuse collection and the working conditions of its employees.

The spirit of enterprise and empathy set her apart from the English children she went to school with, at Bassett House School in Kensington. While most children her age were happily playing, Zerbanoo was thinking of how she could help the financially disadvantaged children.

Before moving to London, she had been affected by the sight of children begging on the streets of Poona. Encouraged to think for herself, she decided to do something to help the deprived children of India. The fact that she was in faraway London, hardly seemed to matter.

Working on her plan, seven-year-old Zerbanoo asked Mappie, her godmother, who in those days worked for the Queen's couturière Hardy Amies, for some fabric and pins.

Mappie watched with fascination as Zerbanoo deftly created little flags with pins and scraps of fabric. Hours later, she stepped out on the pavement outside her family home, Heritage Hotel in London, and stopped every passer-by, offering them a flag in return for a penny. Her enterprise was successful. Soon she had raised £10. Without wasting time, she sealed the money in an envelope and posted it to the official residence of the prime minister of India, Jawaharlal Nehru.

Not long after, she received a letter from the Indian prime minister's office. The letter acknowledged her act of kindness. Pandit Nehru, as he was popularly called, wrote a thank you letter to Zerbanoo saying, 'If every girl in England was like you, there would be fewer poor children in Poona.'

Years later, Zerbanoo would receive the Nehru Centenary Award for her work championing the rights of women, children and minorities; the only woman outside India to be so honoured. This award is presented to Indians for their outstanding contribution to the promotion of international understanding.

Growing up on the cusp of two cultures allowed Zerbanoo to walk the bridge that connected the East and West. During the early fifties in Britain, people had to give their allegiance to one or the other way of living but Zerbanoo deliberately refused to choose. Though she succeeded in maintaining a subtle balance, there were occasions when she got caught in the collision of cultures and was stereotyped by her eastern heritage.

While at Roedean School in Brighton during the seventies, Zerbanoo didn't feel discriminated against. She felt greatly cared for and was fortunate to excel in team sports, especially cricket and lacrosse. She always topped the class in history, a subject that fascinates her to this day. If there was any subtle typecasting, she did not notice it. Today, many of Zerbanoo's most treasured friends are those she made in her school days.

An unplanned encounter with her former school housemistress, Miss Pickering, or 'Pick' as she was nicknamed, at her Care Home in Manchester, was the first intimation she had of having been considered 'different' at school.

Zerbanoo had been invited to be the guest of honour at the start of the series of events commemorating two hundred years of the end of the British Slave Trade in 2007. She travelled by train to give a talk at the Manchester Cathedral on the importance of the historic campaign to end the slave trade and the need to put a stop to modern slavery. Interestingly, two hundred years ago, nearly half the population of Manchester had signed a petition to be presented to Parliament to bring an end to the transatlantic slave trade. This was remarkable, as even today with modern technology, it would be difficult to solicit and engage half the population of Manchester to stop anything. For Zerbanoo, it was the perfect place to remember the plight of the millions who had suffered horrendous inhumanity to satisfy others' greed.

Zerbanoo, as always the bad traveller, had been sick on the train from London to Manchester. The guards took good care of her upon her arrival at Manchester Piccadilly Station, and arranged for her to be at the head of the taxi queue. She had to go to the BBC studios to be interviewed for the evening chat show before her talk at the Cathedral.

On being told by the Pakistani taxi driver that the studio was close by, Zerbanoo realized that she had extra time on hand.

On the spur of the moment, she took a detour to her former housemistress's care home.

It was a meeting that would remain with her for a long time. During their chat, she was taken aback when Pick, who shared her birthday with Zerbanoo told her that she had been waiting all these years to make a confession to her.

Holding on to her hand tightly, she said:

We knew our girls so well and could foretell the script of their future lives. We were seldom, if ever, wrong. We were aware that you were special, but always thought of you as a foreigner with a difficult father who would marry you off early. We presumed you would settle down to a contented married life. So you see, Zerbanoo, you were unique. You were the one that broke our nearly 100 per cent success rate of predicting our girls' futures ... I want to apologize for not giving you the academic attention you deserved. We never thought you would make such a big difference to the world ... I needed to say sorry before I die.

Zerbanoo in her usual candid way responded:

Dearest Pick, you did me a big favour. If you had put me down the purely academic route, I would have never attempted to venture into the unpredictable world of politics. Neither would I have taken myself off on endless adventures around the world. I always felt loved and it was wonderful that no one had any expectations of me, as it gave me the freedom to be myself.

Comforting the teacher who believed she had wronged her, Zerbanoo kissed her goodbye and left. A few weeks later, Pick died.

Often asked by schools to deliver end-of-year talks and give away awards, she recalls that in her speech at her old preparatory school Godstowe, she admitted to teachers, parents and students that she felt a comradeship with all the girls who had never won trophies.

I told them not to feel discouraged because they did not need such tokens to make something of themselves. All they need is spirit and an unyielding belief in their unique purpose. I recalled how I was once fed up at never receiving any accolades in school and complained in my usual straightforward way to the headmistress, Miss Webster. To this she responded, 'The Nightingale never won any prizes at the poultry show.'

FOUR

A LEAP OF FAITH

Almost every girl belonging to the ancient Zoroastrian faith faces a dilemma when she comes of marriageable age. She inevitably walks the tightrope between her faith and fate. A conscious decision has to be made that will determine whether she is going to follow the path of true love or sacrifice it at the altar of religious tradition to maintain the bloodline of one of the oldest religions in the world.

The options are tough considering most young Zoroastrians are zealously brought up to believe that they will eventually marry within the community that is dwindling in numbers.

Unlike other religions, such as Christianity and Islam, which depend on converts to increase numbers, Zoroastrianism has been strictly based on ethnicity. The race depends on its own kind to increase demographics. The ancient religion that had reached the pinnacle of glory during the Persian Empire has always been divided on the issue of accepting inter-faith marriages, and passionate about maintaining the purity of the bloodline. Every parent fervently hopes that their children are fortunate enough to find a life partner who is a Zoroastrian. Alternatively, the eligible bachelorette agrees to an arranged marriage where the parents or family friends do a thorough background check of the prospective Zoroastrian suitor. Those who fail the pedigree test are caught in the crossfire. If a woman dares to break the rule and marries an 'outsider', she could well run the risk of losing face and being ostracized by the inner circle of family, friends and the orthodox heavyweights in the community. The men, however, are exempt from the same trial by fire.

Like every other young girl born in the Zoroastrian faith, following the sacred dictum of good thoughts, good words and good deeds, Zerbanoo had been brought up to believe that someday she would marry her own kind. The well-defined ground rules of marrying a suitable Zoroastrian boy had been dinned into her at an early age. There was no question of crossing the invisible line.

On her twenty-first birthday, Zerbanoo decided to organize a party to celebrate the milestone. The venue was her parent's house in the Wiltshire countryside, near Stonehenge. A stickler for details, she wanted everything to be perfect.

The dress she wore on the big day was a copy of the one worn by Scarlet O'Hara in the movie *Gone with the Wind*. The cake was a symbolic elegant swan with forty cygnets, one for each guest, around the base. The live band had been confirmed. The numbers in the guest list had been meticulously matched to make sure that all her girlfriends had been partnered with suitably gorgeous men.

Just as she was certain that every detail had been taken care of, Zerbanoo received a call. It was from an old family friend who asked to be excused from the party. Zerbanoo was worried as the women now outnumbered the men. Luckily, one of her girlfriends had a solution. She asked her boyfriend to invite his flat mate Richard, another solicitor.

As the guests started arriving, the unexpected happened. A tall, blue-eyed man walked in with his friend. Zerbanoo was quoted in a British magazine which featured their love story: 'It was more than love at first sight, it was a thunderbolt.'

It was *colpo di fulmines* as the Italians would say. Zerbanoo says she experienced a surreal gut feeling that the man she had locked eyes with was her soulmate. An extraordinary feeling of having known the handsome stranger before, perhaps in another lifetime.

Today, more than forty-four years later, their partnership is a study in the fine balance of the yin and the yang. Zerbanoo often paints a larger-than-life collage of how to change the world and instinctively moves very quickly taking on impossible projects. Richard helps her make it happen. He's the glue she needs to stick the big picture on a reality board. Whilst Zerbanoo blows you away with the way she works, Richard is the calming one who is grounded and supportive of everything she does. They share a rock-solid relationship that helps them tide over the tsunamis of life.

Zerbanoo's younger sister, Genie, who is also married to an Englishman, Nick, gives credit to Richard for being the plank of stability in Zerbanoo's life whilst she is busy conquering the world.

My sister wouldn't have been able to achieve so much without Richard's continued support. He's always been there for her.

Whether it was politics, building the ASHA Centre or allowing a constant stream of people to stay at their home, over the years, Richard has always stood by her. Zerbanoo often jumps up in the air and, he catches her with a kiss.

However, unlike now when inter-faith marriages are accepted, society in the early seventies found them a novelty. Zerbanoo found herself being the centre of speculation as she was often interviewed by the media looking for sound bites on the highs and lows of a marriage that broke the norms.

In one of her archived interviews, Zerbanoo was quoted on her first encounter with Richard: 'I just felt that I'd known him for eternity. I thought this is who I have been waiting for.'

Richard was less forthcoming about the first time they met. Zerbanoo shrugs it off as his British reserve. She teases him saying, 'Your ancestors, the Normans, were a bunch of thugs who came for the loot,' but looks rather pleased when referred to as Richard's Norman conquest.

Richard comes from a historical lineage of Normans. His ancestor, Bishop Gifford, headed one of the ten families who came to Britain from Normandy with William the Conqueror in 1066. Bishop Gifford was William the Conqueror's cousin and close adviser. Of the ten original families, only the Maris and Giffords can trace a direct line back to the last time Britain was ever conquered by foreigners.

With her straightforward approach to life, Zerbanoo is open to different ways of understanding the world. When a past life regression practitioner confirmed that Richard was her soulmate, it re-established something she already knew: that Richard has been a big part of her karmic cycle.

Past life therapy technique uses hypnosis to recover what practitioners believe are memories of past incarnations. Zerbanoo was told that they had met in several lifetimes but were not destined to be together as husband and wife until this lifetime. That explained why she felt compelled to marry Richard, despite the strong opposition from her father.

She also found Richard's even temperament particularly endearing. It was an antithesis to her father. While Bailey was an overbearing patriarch, Richard was diametrically opposite with his gentle and indulgent approach. He allowed her to be. She found Richard's sense of humour, sensitivity and intellectual rigour, very attractive.

Richard wooed Zerbanoo by reading poetry to her. He won her over by extending old-fashioned English courtesies and making her laugh. In the early days of their courtship, Richard would test Zerbanoo's knowledge of English literature and quiz her on her extensive general knowledge.

When Zerbanoo later questioned him about this cross-examination, Richard said it was to ensure she had the intelligence to bring up their children. Zerbanoo must have passed with flying colours, considering years later, Mark their older son, studied theology, passed his masters in the study of Indian religions with a first-class distinction and later went on to qualify as a solicitor.

Alexander, their second son, besides being a scholar at the famous Harrow School (where the all-time greats like Lord Byron, Winston Churchill and Pandit Nehru studied), went on to read English at New College, Oxford and is now a writer and theatre director.

Following English tradition, Richard asked Zerbanoo's father for his daughter's hand in marriage. Only to have Bailey bluntly refuse. To illustrate his point, Bailey narrated the Persian tale of the proverbial eagle and the dove that flew happily together. However, when the eagle was hungry, it pounced on the dove and polished it off for lunch.

A little baffled by the outcome of the story, Richard in all earnestness assured his potential father-in-law that his intentions were perfectly honourable. He said he'd never be the eagle who would hurt his daughter in any way. To which Bailey guffawed saying, 'You fool, you are not the eagle ... she is.'

Bailey explained to Richard that, considering his ancestors had kept their faith alive through a millennium of religious persecution, he would never permit his daughter to marry outside the faith. Although Richard understood Bailey's dilemma, he was still determined to marry Zerbanoo.

After giving it some thought, Bailey asked Richard to delay the marriage so they could be sure of their love. Richard agreed. In the meanwhile, Zerbanoo travelled to India and Iran discreetly in search of a suitable boy who belonged to her own race and religion.

After two years of weighing the pros and cons of marriage to each other, Zerbanoo and Richard had a church wedding at St. Mary's on Harrow-on-the-Hill, witnessed by close family and friends. The church was one of the first to be built by the Normans in England after their conquest in the eleventh century. Byron's daughter Allegra lies buried there in an unmarked grave.

Bailey didn't attend the wedding on principle. There were no traditional Zoroastrian wedding rituals. Zerbanoo's uncle Gussie, Bailey's older brother, gave her away. Gussie mentioned in his speech that he'd brought Zerbanoo to England as a little girl to be reunited with her parents and now he was giving her away to a perfect English gentleman. He hoped Richard would take good care of her because she was precious to all her family.

It was a traditional wedding. Richard's school and Cambridge friend, music scholar and composer Christopher Palmer played the organ. Rejecting Handel's *Wedding March* as far too predictable, he played Strauss' *Thus Spake Zarathushtra* as Zerbanoo walked up the aisle on her uncle's arm. The tune had been made popular as the theme to the movie *2001: A Space Odyssey*. He amped it up a bit with a Beatles medley as the couple signed the wedding register.

Although the wedding was picture-perfect, Zerbanoo missed her father's presence. It was the price she had to pay for finding true love. The last thing her father said to her before the wedding was, 'You make your bed and you have to lie in it.'

The newlyweds did have a bed to lie in, but they couldn't afford a sofa (neither did they have a TV, a washing machine or a car). As a newly-articled lawyer from Cambridge, Richard was barely making enough to make ends meet. To make matters worse, they had sunk whatever savings they had into buying a dilapidated cottage on Harrow Hill for £12,750. Most of his earnings went into paying the heavy mortgage. Unfortunately, it wasn't long before the foundation of the house gave way and the edifice began to sink.

Wanting to see how his daughter would manage without his support, Bailey stubbornly refused to give any kind of financial assistance. However, Zerbanoo was determined to ride it out. She was certain they would survive by sheer dint of hard work and hope.

Eventually their Pollyannaism paid off when, months later, an envelope arrived in the post. Zerbanoo wondered if it was yet another bill they couldn't pay. Richard, on the other hand, insisted that whatever it was, they would deal with it. Tearing open the envelope, they discovered Zerbanoo had won a national premium bond! There was just enough money to buy their first sofa.

Coincidence followed luck, and Zerbanoo won her second premium bond. Ernie, the mascot for the British Lottery Premium Bonds Board, had again picked her numbers. Twice lucky … This time it allowed the young couple to buy a car.

Even when the times were tough, Zerbanoo would give a percentage of their income to charity. She says, 'I always felt that ten per cent belongs to God and he expects you to give to others in His name especially when He sends you a gift.'

Zerbanoo also reveals that marrying Richard was the best decision she ever made. In her words, 'He is an exceptional husband and friend. Richard has encouraged me to express my potential. Few men have the confidence to allow their wives to do that.'

Although Bailey occasionally wished that Richard was an eccentric Zoroastrian instead of a perfect Englishman, he finally accepted him into the family fold. Regardless of Richard's genealogy, Bailey was shrewd enough to know that it helped to have a lawyer in the family who could aid him with the legalities of the properties he owned. That too, without charging a penny!

Word was that Bailey kept a secret stash of Richard's legal correspondence that he thought was brilliant. Bailey would discreetly read his son-in-law's legal letters over and over again to grasp the finer nuances of Richard's cleverly-worded communication with his clients.

Despite marrying outside the community, Zerbanoo strongly recommends that every young Zoroastrian should marry within the folds of the ancient religion to continue being the flag-bearers of the proud race.

The irony of it was when one of her Zoroastrian girlfriends living in London called up to have a chat. In the midst of the conversation she let slip that she was afraid to inform Zerbanoo about her son dating an English girl. 'Only because I know how strongly you feel about the issue of marrying outside the community!' she said by way of explanation.

FIVE

THE WINNER TAKES IT ALL

It was a typical Monday morning in the winter of 1981, when a knock on the door of Zerbanoo's beautiful Victorian home in London interrupted her morning routine – a part of the homemaker's ritual of cooking, cleaning and caring for her family. Minutes later, only too happy to take a break, she was having a conversation with two men at her doorstep.

They were activists in search of an ideal location to showcase their Liberal party posters. Upon spotting the magnificent old ash tree that stood in the front garden of Zerbanoo's home at the top of the famous Harrow Hill, the party workers thought it was an ideal spot for their political banner.

The politicians asked Zerbanoo for her permission. She agreed, half expecting them to give up the pursuit since climbing the tree seemed like an impossible task. To her surprise, the men resourcefully returned with a ladder and managed to fix the poster at a vantage point.

Zerbanoo was impressed and invited them in. Over tea and biscuits, she questioned them about the Liberal party's views on various topics like childcare and public transport. She wanted definitive answers as she had written letters to local politicians asking for affordable and accessible early childcare but none of her appeals had been answered.

Spurred by the avid interest she was showing in party issues, one of the men casually asked Zerbanoo if she would like to contest the forthcoming local elections scheduled for May 1982. Even before she had a chance to assimilate the information, he made it crystal clear that she should not harbour any false notions of winning a safe Conservative seat saying, 'All we need is a paper candidate. We'll put your name on the ballot paper; Harrow has a growing ethnic minority vote and you will make the party look more diverse and inclusive.'

In the early eighties, women were still hopelessly under-represented in British politics. It was a rarity to find a woman, least of all a young British-Indian mother, contesting elections. Shrewd enough to know that a woman of Zerbanoo's calibre and background would add gloss to the party image, the men also wanted her to understand that the role of women in politics was mainly to make tea, raise funds and deliver political leaflets.

John Lennon's famous line, 'Life happens when you are busy making other plans,' applied perfectly to the young Zerbanoo. Although busy looking after her family, studying for an Open University degree with no plans at all of becoming a politician, Zerbanoo took on the challenge. Despite being a novice, she knew she would learn on the job. After all, there were no professional qualifications or training required to be a politician.

Keeping in mind her father's oft given advice, a famous Grantland Rice quote:

For when the One Great Scorer comes
To mark against your name,
He writes – not that you won or lost –
But how you played the Game

Zerbanoo jumped into the political arena. She knew she had nothing to lose and that she may even enjoy the game of politics.

Her entry into politics was one more in a series of well-timed incidents that opened up new opportunities. The most significant one had happened when she was just twenty and was working for one of the top advertising agencies in the world, Foote, Cone and Belding, in their new ideas department at Baker Street, London. She had a lateral mind, was street savvy and a hard worker.

I had spent the previous year on a postgraduate course qualifying in advertising and marketing, and then landed this fabulous job. One afternoon, I was asked to deliver a letter to a client's office at the Strand in central London. Going up in the lift, I got off on the wrong floor but knocked on the right door. It opened up a new vista for me. It was the office of the newly formed national charity Shelter. I started a casual conversation with the lady at the reception and was so impressed by the work they did for the homeless that I immediately signed up as a volunteer.

Without wasting much time, she took the initiative of organizing volunteer groups around London. Returning home from a fundraising meeting one evening, she noticed an empty building on Chapel Street near the Edgware Road Station. It would make an ideal Shelter charity shop that could be run by the homeless themselves. She was convinced that the idea had real potential. It would help the homeless and at the same time, the less well-off could buy second-hand clothes and household goods that people were willing to donate to charity.

Inspired by the detective Sherlock Holmes, whose home is supposed to be in the area next to the advertising agency that she worked in at Baker Street, Zerbanoo deduced that it was elementary that an empty building near a major tube station must belong to the London Transport.

The head of properties for London Transport was clearly taken aback when a young girl walked into his office, naïvely asking if she could have the empty building for work with the homeless, with no concrete plans about how she was going to pay for it. His first reaction was to knock the idea on the head and tell Zerbanoo that the property was due for redevelopment. Thinking quickly on her feet, Zerbanoo asked if she could use the property as a charity shop for a few weeks until the demolition work started. Within minutes, the deal was settled with a promise to move out of the premises the instant London Transport needed to start work on the building. It was the first of many charity shops that she would set up. Zerbanoo's younger brother Naswan still remembers going to the launch of the third Shelter shop near their home in Queensway, London, as a young boy. She had invited Polly James of the *Liver Birds* (a television programme that was topping the charts at the time), to cut the ribbon. Even at that time, Zerbanoo was savvy enough to connect with influential people and involve them in charity work.

The following three years were spent collecting funds for the homeless, organizing volunteers, launching supporter groups, coordinating publicity and making speeches about the damaging consequences of not having a home of one's own. It would prove to be a valuable training ground for politics. In her words: 'My years at Shelter gave me invaluable insight into the lives of the homeless and their sufferings.'

She also picked up organizational and fundraising skills that were useful to her later in her political life.

A sense of optimistic spontaneity pushed her to take the plunge into the world of politics. The only way to start was to go knocking on people's doors to introduce herself to the voters. With three-year-old Alexander, nick-named Wags, in a pushchair, she set about getting to know everyone in her constituency. She asked them about the changes they would like to see in their locality. Wags turned out to be a great ice-breaker. Zerbanoo spent the entire campaign meeting the cross-section of the community that stayed at home during the day: mainly pensioners, mothers, the unemployed and night-college students. It gave her a definite edge over the other candidates who would meet voters in the evenings, when they were tired after a day's work and would be thinking of supper and television, rather than listening to vote-seeking politicians. The 'friendly, pushchair mum' and 'agony aunt' patiently heard everyone out. Soon she was known as the lovely Asian lady with a smiling baby. Much later, Zerbanoo would joke that it was only because of Wags she won the popularity polls.

Zerbanoo connected with most people in her constituency. Yet there were residents who were extremely hostile and spat at her saying, 'We will never vote for a blackie!' Despite the humiliation, all Zerbanoo did was return home and wash herself with cleansing salt water. The following day she would bravely step out again to campaign on the same street.

Such venomous attacks would have disheartened anyone else, but her upbringing in Britain gave her an understanding of how racial prejudice, be it subtle or overt, worked. Zerbanoo knew that her maiden name 'Irani' was a disadvantage, especially when it came to job interviews. In contrast, there were plenty of polite call-backs as soon as she took on the Gifford name after marriage. There was no denying that racism was a reality in Britain of the early eighties.

The world of politics at the time was also an unequal one for British Asian women. Members of the Liberal party, who were initially convinced that it was a 'politically correct' move to get an Asian woman on board, did not canvass with her. She recalls how she pushed herself to continue, keeping in mind the ideal of US President Theodore Roosevelt who believed that it didn't matter if you failed, as long as you failed while daring greatly so that your place was never with the cold and timid souls who knew neither victory nor defeat.

The odds were against her; however, fate had a surprise in store. The election results left everyone dumbfounded. 'It just can't be possible,' was the collective reaction. Zerbanoo had won by five votes! It was a historic victory. With a landside twenty-seven per cent swing, she had defeated Major Harsant of the Tory party, to become the first Asian woman to ever win a seat for the Liberal party in Britain.

It was a safe Tory seat. My own party couldn't believe I had won and that the other two Liberals also standing for the seat in Ridgeway had lost. They called for a recount. The last thing anyone expected was that my vote would go up. Then the Tories called for a recount. We were told that that would have to wait until the next day as everyone was tired and needed to go home to bed. On Friday morning, we returned for another recount. It ended up as the only count in the whole of London. The Tory party's call for another recount ended with my vote going up to fifteen votes. Then they called for a recount and the total went up to twenty-two votes. It was a media circus. After which the election officer said, 'Mrs Gifford has won. There will be no more recounts.'

Political observers saw traces of similarity with Dadabhai Naoroji, known as the Grand Old Man of India, who had won his seat in 1892 as a Liberal by precisely five votes. His vote was also contested, and after some legal wrangles he entered parliament as the first non-white to be elected to the British parliament. He was later nicknamed 'Mr Narrow Majority' as people found it difficult to pronounce his foreign name.

Zerbanoo's flamboyant presence in an otherwise drab world of political men was also keenly watched. Being the only Liberal woman councillor along with the dozen Liberal men, she promptly earned the sobriquet 'the thirteenth man'.

The press was supportive of the female candidate. Thousands of neatly filed press cuttings speak volumes of her being acclaimed by the media. She was a refreshing change with a photogenic face, representing hope against the backdrop of predictable politics. In contrast to the grey politicians, Zerbanoo was a bright young thing, a happily married mother committed to public service. Her career became the symbol of a woman's ability to dovetail the personal with the political. She asserted the fundamental truth that power is gender free.

Her entry into the boys' club was a tough one. Seeing how

vulnerable and inexperienced Zerbanoo was, June King, a former politician, took her aside and gave her some good advice. The former mayor spoke about the importance of the first impression being the lasting one.

> The first time you speak, people will be assessing your intellectual calibre so talk on a subject you have an in-depth knowledge of. The other politicians and council officers will be firing questions at you, which you must answer and be well-informed on. They will be judging every word. Secondly, always dress impeccably. Men just change their ties and wear the same old suit. A woman is judged every day on her appearance, as it is a sexist world. Just look fabulous.

Zerbanoo took the advice seriously. On her very first entrance into the council chamber, she donned a classic cream raw silk Nehru jacket and a fitted A-line skirt, distinctly standing out from the Liberal party men known for their 'T-shirt and sandals'. Zerbanoo soon had the media talking about her innate sense of style. Some years later, she was chosen by the fashion design students at Westminster University as the politician for whom they wished to design clothes during their final year project. Zerbanoo wore the outfits created by them all through the general election campaign of 1987, and the winning outfit on television for the Liberal Alliance Party Political Broadcast. Swedish television covered her campaign as the winning design student was Swedish.

Keeping June King's wise words in mind, Zerbanoo didn't speak up in the first few council meetings. It led to the Mayor patronizingly asking her in a deliberate, slow manner, 'Do you speak English, Mrs Gifford?' Zerbanoo responded, saying, 'How do you think I won the elections? Do you think I spoke Double Dutch?' Her repartee evoked laughter and drove home the fact that she wasn't one to take snide remarks lying down.

When she finally took the floor, she delivered a powerful, well-researched speech on housing problems and the need for Harrow to have a Housing Aid Centre. Up until then, Harrow was one of the few boroughs in London that did not have a centre to help the homeless. Having worked at the homeless charity Shelter, it was a subject close to her heart. Her speech was followed by a rapid-fire question-and-answer session that she handled with the ease of a professional. Nevertheless, it was not a cakewalk.

My speeches met with catcalls and rowdiness familiar to anyone listening to the prime minister's question time in the House of Commons. When that failed to unsettle me, my presence would be ignored and the chairman would deliberately look surprised if I wished to make any contribution to the meeting. It was so puerile, the way they made me feel unwelcome and out of place.

Giving up was simply never an option. A fighter, she continued to challenge the status quo, taking up cudgels on behalf of those who were marginalized or ignored. It meant starting with small gestures that made a big difference to people. Zerbanoo found herself in a privileged position to write letters and speak to the right people in order to make good things happen for those sidelined by society.

People turned to her for help knowing it would be forthcoming.

When the council refused to spend the extra money required to install a bath so that a disabled eighteen-year-old could bathe himself, instead of being helped by his aged grandmother in the shower, Zerbanoo ensured he got his bath.

There was so much to learn as a newly-minted politician. She learnt the details of council procedures, how to chair a committee and the intricacies of the law. It involved burning the midnight oil voraciously reading countless briefings. Life was a whirl of endless meetings, speeches, briefs and guest appearances. She talked, dined and corresponded not only with grassroots community leaders but also with bureaucrats, diplomats, academics; learning how to deal with issues across a wide social spectrum. It was a huge learning curve which required dynamism and incisive intelligence. Zerbanoo admitted:

I had never written a political press release or spoken on public platforms before winning the election. Nor did I know how to answer political questions, be it on television or radio. I had to learn not only the Liberal policy but also Labour and Conservative policies. Politics throws up the unexpected. So many things can happen. You have to be able to handle any crisis and be on top of every brief and have a view on everything. That is very terrifying as no one can do all that. Too much is asked of politicians. But what they should be asked is to be honest and not corrupt and to actually act for the wellbeing of all the community and not just their mates.

Close friends who rallied around her remember how she orchestrated her political campaigns from her kitchen table at her home, Herga House in Harrow. They recollect the frantic days when friends, family and neighbours were roped in to help with the promise of a hearty meal. Friend Shirley McVoy even moved into the Gifford home for three weeks in 1986 to help look after her boys when Zerbanoo was travelling to America as a guest of the US government on their visitors' programme.

As a rising star in British politics, Zerbanoo was invited to tour the United States. The trip has been etched in her mind as one of the most stimulating experiences of her life. She loved America and the fact that everything was possible there for somebody who worked hard to make a difference. In her words, 'In Britian if you tried ten new ideas and nine were successful, but one was a failure, people would think you were a disaster. In contrast, in America, if you tried ten new ideas and nine failed, but one was brilliant, you were a success story.'

Meeting everyone from senators and civil rights activists, to having important briefings with power brokers in the Pentagon and lunching with Edward Koch, Mayor of New York, was an exhilarating experience. Zerbanoo spent time with the women's campaign fund in Washington, learning how American women were working together to ensure more women were supported when they stood for public office. It didn't matter whether they were Democrat or Republican. There was so much to learn about funding a successful campaign and picking up the finer nuances of dealing with the media.

The three weeks that her friend Shirley was meant to live in Harrow, looking after Mark and Alexander whilst Zerbanoo toured America, turned into a year. Shirley's daughter, Marigold, was one of the only two girls who were awarded a scholarship to study at the famous Harrow boys' school. She wanted to be close to the school and the Gifford home was perfectly situated. Shirley says she can never forget those endless meals that she baked for volunteers who were helping with Zerbanoo's parliamentary campaign in Harrow East in 1987. She recalls, 'Cooking for the elections meant just one meal, baked potatoes. They were hot and could be filled with any extras like cheese, tuna or corn and butter. I know that thanks to those endless trays of baked potatoes, I'll never eat another one in my life.'

Shirley also remembers how she once made Richard laugh his head off by observing that, in most political campaigns there were too many chiefs and not enough Indians but, 'In Zerbanoo's political campaign, there were too many Indians and not enough chiefs.'

Election time was corybantic. Friends distributed election leaflets in the neighbourhood and everyone pitched in. Even Zerbanoo's mother, Kitty, stood outside supermarkets asking people to vote for her daughter.

Politics was something I was not involved with before I became a campaigner for Zerbanoo. I was proud to ask everyone to vote for her. I told them that she is incorruptible, fearless and a tireless crusader against injustice. She will be your champion and not rest until the job is done.

'Zerbanoo has a disarming way of getting things done,' points out Richard who willingly became her election agent. 'It was stressful times for all of us,' he says of this chaotic but memorable phase of their lives. Richard had his hands full running the campaign, keeping track of the expenditure and the legalities of an election campaign. It also involved putting up posters wherever they got permission to do so. He must have done a good job because Zerbanoo won the poster war. There were beautiful photographs of her smiling back from every vantage point in the borough of Harrow.

Rising to the challenge of politics, Zerbanoo took the dramatic highs and lows in her stride. She was quoted in the *Sunday Times*, 'Politics requires a lot of guts.' She continued with her usual humour to compare an election campaign to a workout. 'Women go to aerobics classes to lose weight. They should go on an election campaign.' The political experience also gave her the quiet strength to tackle the bully boys who tried to intimidate her.

SIX

BULLY BOYS

There was a time when Zerbanoo almost crumbled under the onslaught of racist threats to destroy her. She seriously contemplated giving up public life for her young family.

Murmurs of discontent started doing the rounds when Zerbanoo was named as the prospective Liberal Alliance Parliamentary candidate for Hertsmere in 1983. Always game for a fair fight, she challenged the chairman of the Tory party, Cecil Parkinson for his safe seat. This was the same powerful Cecil Parkinson who was appointed minister in Margaret Thatcher's first government in 1979. As one of Margaret Thatcher's favourites, he was poised to be Britain's Foreign Secretary, after the general election of 1983.

Cecil Parkinson's career stalled after the general election when the news of his secretary, Sara Keays, being pregnant with his love child hit the headlines. It was presumed by the media that he would resign. This would lead to a parliamentary by-election. It was assumed that one of the 'gang of four', who had recently left the Labour party and created the new Social

Democratic Party and were now in alliance with the Liberals, would stand at that by-election, as it would give them a good chance of being re-elected to parliament. The hierarchy of the SDP/Liberal Alliance were astounded when the local Hertsmere members refused to have anyone parachuted in. If there was to be a stunning victory that would trounce their rivals, Zerbanoo was to be their candidate. They made this clear by making her the president of the Hertsmere constituency.

Parkinson did not resign. Zerbanoo never got to fight a by-election.

Zerbanoo recalls the night of the count in Hertsmere, on 09 June 1983, and the abruptness of Parkinson towards her and the Labour candidate. As Parkinson was heir elect to Thatcher, it was being televised as one of the important counts in Britain. Zerbanoo was confronted by cameras and asked what she felt about the rudeness of Cecil Parkinson. She answered in her usual uncensored way saying that Parkinson would have to learn diplomacy before he became Foreign Secretary. Parkinson never held high office again.

After contesting the Hertsmere seat for the alliance, in a forty-day campaign trail, Zerbanoo came second to Cecil Parkinson. Although she received the highest number of votes won by any ethnic minority candidate in Britain, pushing the Labour party into third place, she lost the election. Her vote represented an eighteen per cent swing to the alliance. It was, in political terms, a landslide victory and unheard of for a virgin politician in the national arena. Yet the harsh reality of the political campaign was not known to the general public until much later. Zerbanoo had not allowed the media to report the story of the racism and intimidation she suffered during the election campaign as she wanted to contest the seat on her own merits.

It was only later that the *Mail on Sunday* newspaper report titled *My Nightmare of Race Terror* broke the news about the sustained campaign of racial terrorization that was launched to psyche Zerbanoo out of the political arena during election time.

The report stated that upon first hearing the story about the police mounting a guard on the Gifford's residence to prevent her from being assaulted, the *Mail on Sunday* contacted Zerbanoo for a personal interview. Hesitant to talk to the press, she only later opened up to the media. Up until then, she had been reluctant to speak about the agony she and her family had undergone.

Even during the 1982 local election campaign in Harrow, she had suffered the humiliation of leaflets being circulated asking residents to refrain from voting for her because she was a 'black foreigner'. Determined not to give undue publicity to the racists, Zerbanoo ignored the pressure tactics and fought the election on her own merit. She won that election by a landslide.

It was only after the 1983 general election in Hertsmere that she allowed the media to release the shocking story of the violent racism she had suffered.

The terrifying account of her being shadowed and attacked sounded like a script of a horror movie. It was late, and Zerbanoo was home alone when the phone rang, shattering the stillness of the night. Richard was away with their sons in Norwich visiting his parents. Zerbanoo was in the bath, trying to unwind after a hard day of campaigning. She jumped out of the bath and picked up the receiver to hear a man's voice at the other end snarl, 'We know you are alone. We are not going to let Asians run this country, we are coming in to get you and we are coming through the greenhouse.' So saying, he slammed the phone down.

Zerbanoo went cold knowing she was being watched. The threat was real. How else would they know she was alone that night and that the first floor conservatory led to her bedroom? The conservatory, which was at the back of the house, could not be seen from the main road.

She quickly dialled 999. The police arrived within minutes. At first, the police looked sceptical until they answered the phone themselves and heard the vicious threat. Zerbanoo was given police protection. A police woman kept her company through the night.

The nasty calls continued even after that fateful night. They occurred intermittently every two or three days with the callers hurling racial abuse. The abusive garbage flung at her ranged from dangerous warnings to kidnap her sons alternated by crude threats of sexual assault. Her detractors wanted her out of public life and were willing to go to any lengths to push her off the political stairway. A series of scary incidents perpetuating terror, followed.

One evening, Zerbanoo was shocked to find a masked man slashing the side door with a knife. Her frantic screams drove him away. Fortunately, there were other people with her on that particular day who helped her handle the stressful situation. Another time, when she was driving home late at night after an official meeting, she realized a car was shadowing her. It tried to force her off the road by ramming into the side of her car at high speed.

Later that evening, she received a sinister call saying her

car had been tampered with and it was dangerous to drive it. The following night, her car windows were smashed and a threatening note was found telling her to get out of politics and go back to where she came from. In a newspaper report, Zerbanoo had said, 'There were a spate of abusive phone calls from thugs threatening to flog me, rape me and kill me if I went ahead with my political career.'

Her way of coping with the intrusion was to install burglar alarms and laser beams to detect intruders and floodlight her home.

We lit the house all night and put bars on all windows. We had a panic button installed in the main rooms. It was a tough decision but I decided to go on. When I first stood for local government in 1982 in Harrow, the National Front bully boys put leaflets around the council estates saying decent English folk shouldn't be voting for a non-English person. The press contacted me then but at that time, I simply felt that any story would just publicize the racists. I wanted to starve them of publicity, to deny them credibility. It was Sue Douglas, then known as the Queen of Fleet Street who convinced me to allow my story to be told. She was at my home having dinner after the general election in Hertsmere in 1983. She witnessed the misery of being a target of sick racists. Sue persuaded me to go public. She was of the opinion that it was high time people realized that racist attacks didn't just happen only to Asians in Brick Lane as the public thought it to be. It happened to anyone who did not fit the narrow view of the white supremacists.

Decent British people needed to know what was happening in their country.

As the sensational story of how Zerbanoo was attacked by the 'Merchants of Hate' hit the stands, the press hailed her as a heroine. The national papers in Britain and India acknowledged the personal and political triumph with a slew of headlines describing her as 'A Caring 24-Carat Campaigner', 'Fighting for Others' Rights', and 'A Woman of Substance'.

On one occasion, when Zerbanoo was on the BBC's flagship political programme *Question Time* with the former prime minister of Ireland, Tory home secretary, Kenneth Baker, and the Labour firebrand, Clare Short, the abusive telephone calls never seemed to stop. There were so many calls from all over England threatening a blackie for having the audacity to sit next to the British home secretary, that even the police seemed overwhelmed.

It was soon clear that the racists had also infiltrated British Telecom to intercept calls to the Gifford home. This only strengthened Richard's resolve to stand his ground. He had no doubt that his wife should continue in public life. He made a note of every suspicious incident in a document that clearly pointed at right wing extremists. He admitted to the *Daily Express*: 'Zerbanoo knows of the risks when an Asian woman has a high profile career. She is facing up to them bravely. Although it saddens both of us, I am extremely proud of her.'

Archived newspaper cuttings reveal that Bailey, Zerbanoo's father, also stood as an SDP (Social Democratic Party) local candidate in the Hyde Park ward in 1982. He didn't win the council seat but understood how political life worked. It was difficult for him to see his daughter attacked by a bunch of cowards who believed in underhand tactics. Zerbanoo recounts the time he sat her down to advise her. He had said, 'Sweetheart, no one will think ill of you if you step down. You have a young family and you need to protect them. You've gone beyond the call of duty and your winning has no consequence. It is your safety that everyone worries about.'

Although his words suggested that his daughter should look after her personal safety first, Bailey understood the gravity of the situation. He was well aware that surrendering to the narrow-minded racists would send the wrong signals. He realized that if Zerbanoo gave in, it would take a long time for Asians to stand for elections again in their adopted country.

Bailey believed that Zerbanoo's stand was symbolic. An Asian woman contesting a parliamentary seat in the early eighties in Britain demonstrated that, whatever the outcome of the polls, Asians were there to stay. Zerbanoo was a doughty trailblazer whom future generations could follow. If she fought with courage she would be writing a new chapter in the history of Asian women in British politics. Bailey quoted Harper Lee's *To Kill a Mocking Bird*: 'Real courage is when you know you're licked before you begin, but you begin anyway and see it through no matter what.'

Rustom, Zerbanoo's younger brother, who has also been involved with the pulsating world of media and politics, draws out a cluster of memories coloured by the dark days of terror.

I was worried about the racial violence and the death threats Zerbanoo faced. She was often in the papers and on television in those days. My friends at Cambridge used to ask me if I was her brother. I would tell them that she is my sister. Now as a father of young twins I fully appreciate the fact that Zerbanoo used to go campaigning with Alexander in a pushchair. I realize how difficult it must have been for her in those days.

A radio and television journalist himself, Rustom has travelled extensively for the BBC documentary series, *Water Wars*, filmed in Israel and West Bank, Jordan, Turkey and Syria. Rustom has had his share of challenging assignments including the London Weekend Television *Special Inquiry* series on Middle East politics and the programmes on the first war against Iraq titled *War in the Gulf.*

He has also had a brush with politics as the adviser and assistant to the MP Tom King when he was chair of the Intelligence and Security Defence Committee. Tom King, now a life peer, is Baron King of Bridgwater.

Offering a quick analysis of the societal power structure in those days, Rustom explained the social context in which his sister played a stellar role in British politics:

There used to be the upper class, the middle class and the so-called lower class in those days and then there came a class called the 'Celebrity class'. It sort of covered pop stars and celebs in different walks of life. That class transcended all classes. My sister belonged to that celebrity class where she could connect with everyone. She's always been uniquely charismatic and forthright. Perhaps, coming from a race of strong-willed Zoroastrian Iranians who were determined and dynamic, could have contributed to her resolute willpower to battle on. Zerbanoo has the ability to see humour in life's absurdities, which has helped her deal with the stress and petty games that people play.

Being able to laugh at oneself has been an attribute that has served her well. Zerbanoo was rather amused at discovering a spoof leaflet doing the rounds in Harrow. It now has a place of pride alongside her fleet of awards on her mantelpiece. The picture of a blond bombshell with a piece of cloth barely covering her modesty has a tiny typeface running below that reads:

Meet your Liberal Councillor, Zerbanoo Gifford. Zerbanoo Gifford seen here addressing the last Liberal Party Conference at Budleigh Salterton is worthy of support. Educated at Roedean and Barnsley University, Zerbanoo holds several degrees and is qualified at Law. In 1979, she renounced politics and joined the Liberal party and for the last three years has campaigned fearlessly for her ward on the local council; it was largely through her efforts that the Harrow Council recently agreed to supply free skateboards to the borough's Senior Citizens. She lives in the heart of Harrow practically at the top of the famous hill and has been personally responsible for expelling several vampires who had taken up residence in the historic churchyard. For this she has been personally vilified by several Conservative councillors, who saw it as a personal attack on their leader, Mrs Thatcher. That can't be bad by anyone's standards, so carry on Zerbanoo.

She took their advice and happily carried on.

Another telling incident happened earlier on in her political career. A Liberal party member took it upon himself to show Zerbanoo the fine art of canvassing. He asked her to accompany him and watch closely as he approached people in her constituency for their votes. Unfortunately, no one was willing to hear him out.

Every door he knocked on was slammed shut in their faces. Frustrated, Zerbanoo requested the now less confident politician if she could approach the next person. Fortunately for them, the lady of the house invited them in. The first question Zerbanoo asked her was why did everyone slam the door shut on them. The lady looked a little embarrassed as she picked up the phone to ask her neighbour if she knew why every house down the street had refused to entertain the duo. Much to their surprise they got to know that it was a case of mistaken identity. Everyone had presumed that the man with the umbrella knocking on their doors was a Jehovah's Witness, intent on preaching.

Also recounted in neatly filed cuttings are some of the dirty games her political rivals played, including the time they tried to draw a parallel between Zerbanoo and Pamella Bordes who had shot to notoriety, in the mid-eighties, as the girlfriend of Britain's rich and powerful politicians and editors. By virtue of being an Indian, there was a dedicated effort to rub off Pamella's infamous image onto her squeaky clean reputation. Zerbanoo recalls how outrageous it was when, during a parliamentary selection in Twickenham, one of the few winnable Liberal seats, she was asked by an activist in the audience how she could expect others to campaign for her if people mistook her for Pamella Bordes.

Also among the cuttings was a thoughtful letter that Zerbanoo received during the 1987 general election. It illustrated the true dilemma many felt a generation ago at having to vote for a foreign-born politician. This is not such an issue in the Britain of today as voters are now used to living in a multicultural society and seeing non-whites holding power.

The letter stated in clear, bold handwriting:

Why on earth do you want me to vote for Mrs Gifford? She is popular, I can see that. Energetic too, it seems. But the fact remains she is a foreigner and I want to be governed by English (born and bred) people. I understand she has already been on the Harrow Council, so why cannot she be satisfied with that? She has two youngish children to care for as well. I know if I were in her place, I would not have enough energy left over to be an MP as well ... So you have put me and a lot of other folk in a spot.

Princess Usha Devi Rathore, from the Indian royal family of Burdwan, recalls Zerbanoo's enthusiasm and zing even as she dealt day in and day out with all the corruption, lies and nastiness of politics.

In spite of all the hardships, Zerbanoo brought joy and laughter into all our lives. She was like a human dynamo inspiring people and shaking them out of their apathy. I remember her enthusiasm as she invited me on to the board of CRAM (Centre for Research into Asian Migration) that she was helping to start at Warwick University. Zerbanoo involved us all in fundraising, organizing charity balls, getting sponsors until the centre was established. Having come from India, I had never given much thought to immigrants and the Asian diaspora in Britain. The aim of the centre was to put on record the hitherto unknown and often ignored facts relating to the contributions, past and present, made by Asians to countries throughout the world, in which they settled, and especially England. Every project Zerbanoo took on and involved us all in had a definitive purpose to enlighten and educate people. Zerbanoo is as delicate and refined as bone china but the next moment as tough as a tiger taking on the political bully boys. According to the Chinese calendar, Zerbanoo is a rare 'Golden tiger' known for its courage, strong will and fearlessness. The 'golden tiger' only appears every sixty years.

SEVEN

SUCCESS AND SETBACKS

In 1984, Zerbanoo took over as chair of the Community Relations Panel from Lord Avebury, who had held the post for fourteen years. The Liberal party always voted with a fair proportional representation system to ensure that everyone's vote counted. If no one won outright on the first ballot, then second preferences were vital to ensure victory. When the committee voted for a new chair it was safely assumed that all the members probably voted for themselves first and then added Zerbanoo's name as the second preference. Zerbanoo's appointment as the new chair of the Community Relations Panel came as a surprise to everyone including herself.

Zerbanoo decided to celebrate with a grand farewell dinner at the National Liberal Club in London. It was a way of saying thank you to Lord Avebury. The glittering soirée was attended by the heavy-weights of the Liberal party together with the media. Making a special appearance was Joe Grimond, the former leader of the Liberals, and his wife Laura, the granddaughter of a former Liberal prime minister, H.H. Asquith. The Maharaja of Baroda, a friend of Zerbanoo's, also graced the evening in support of her new appointment.

Seated at the head of the table was none other than Lord David Steel, the then Liberal party leader. When it was time for him to make an after dinner speech, he held up the menu that showed Councillor Gifford had been proclaimed the new chair of the Community Relations Panel. He announced with a twinkle in his eye, 'A chair is something you sit on and you try sitting on Zerbanoo,' much to the amusement of everyone.

Although said with humour, the message was loud and clear. Zerbanoo was not one to be walked on, pushed over and most certainly not sat upon. With his trademark Scottish wit and brand of shrewdness, David Steel continued by suggesting that in Scotland someone in her position would be called 'Madame Convener', indeed a more appropriate title for her.

As Chair of the Community Relations Panel, Zerbanoo was determined to do everything in her power to actively formulate and champion policies concerning the ethnic minority communities. She started by closely examining human rights issues, immigration and policing problems that needed immediate attention. Recommendations were made on the need to make the diverse communities feel more settled and welcomed in Britain. It was vital to acknowledge their contributions. All the findings were being factored into party policy.

As the only ethnic minority woman on the panel, Zerbanoo decided to shift the gender balance. She asked the panel members if she could invite more women onto the committee. It would bring a new, vital energy and experience that was needed if the committee were to really effect lasting change.

The response was lukewarm. The excuse was that the people she proposed did not match up to the experience required by the august body.

Desperate to introduce change, she then did something unheard of, although well within the rules of chairing such a committee. She exercised the chairman's prerogative and dissolved it. She then swiftly co-opted new members who wanted to contribute to party policy. Many of these people, who were given their chance to shine through her bold initiative, are among today's high-flyers.

Zerbanoo's roomy attic houses enormous filing cabinets holding systematically archived material: the result of long hours of work put in by the meticulous Lucie Klein from Strasbourg University along with student volunteers Jeff (from Mulhouse University, France), Charlotte (from Mainz University, Germany) and Gesine (from Luneburg University, Germany). Neatly labelled letters, cards, press cuttings and photographs spell out an intricate tapestry of memories of earlier days. The documents are proof of Zerbanoo's thirst for social justice and an unrelenting effort to challenge and change the views of those who supported the status quo. Some, intensely personal missives, reflect a deep commitment to multiple causes that border on modern feminism.

They also included a great amount of private notes validating Zerbanoo's role in promoting the carefully constructed image of the former leader of the Liberal Democrats, Paddy Ashdown. As adviser to Paddy Ashdown on race relations and equality, in the late eighties and early nineties, she was adept at showcasing him impeccably to the many and diverse ethnic minority communities that make up modern Britain.

When it came to dealing with the Indian community, Paddy Ashdown had the distinct advantage of being born in New Delhi into a family of soldiers and police officers who had spent their lives in India since the time of Robert Clive. It suited him to play the ethnic card to raise his game and woo the easy to please, rich minority communities. Zerbanoo, on her part, used her extraordinary network of contacts to garner support for Ashdown. Her circle included around seventeen influential Asian businessmen featured in the list of the wealthiest Asians at that time, who were ready to support Ashdown's election campaign by flying him around the country. Then the media got hold of the gossip of Ashdown's extramarital affairs. 'In an era rife with sex scandals, "Paddy Pantsdown", the most memorable political nickname of our times,' published the *Daily Mail* in a review of the autobiography *Memoirs of a Minor Public Figure* penned by the founder of the charity Shelter and the Liberal party president, Des Wilson. He gave a blow-by-blow account of Paddy Ashdown's infamous affair with his secretary creating havoc among his friends, colleagues and those closest to him in the run up to the 1992 general election.

The sexual exploitation of women in politics infuriated Zerbanoo. The idealist in her believes that true leaders should be noble and inspire others to greatness. She firmly believes, 'They should be people of true moral calibre and not stooges, spivs, sycophants and certainly not sex maniacs.'

There were a number of occasions when Zerbanoo was tempted to blow the whistle about the double standards of the world she inhabited. Instead, she reminded herself that she had stepped into the shoddy world of politics to spearhead positive changes in the community.

Other courageous individuals will expose the stupidity and short-sightedness of men whose only legacy will be their arrogance and immorality. Throughout the world, right thinking people are finding the strength to question the corrupt and disreputable behaviour of these politicians. Everywhere change is in the air.

People whose lives Zerbanoo has touched expressed their dismay at the way she has been treated by the British establishment and particularly her own Liberal party. Many articulated the disappointment that someone of her calibre and commitment to other's welfare should have been deliberately overlooked and sidelined.

Zerbanoo, in her usual straightforward way, sets the record straight.

When David Steel was leader of the Liberal party he did put me forward in 1986 for a Damehood. It was usual practice that the wishes of a party leader were granted but in my case Mrs Thatcher, the then prime minister, turned me down with the excuse that I was too young. At that time, the media reported news of an averted plane crash over North London, headlining it, 'Near Miss over Stanmore'. Richard in his usual humorous way referred to my illusive honour as Near Dame over Stanmore as it was in my constituency.

Some years later, in early 1990, when Zerbanoo was advising the then leader of the Liberals, Paddy Ashdown, she had single-handedly organized a fundraising dinner for twenty potential donors in parliament. Ashdown had told Zerbanoo that he would send her to the House of Lords in recognition of her years of outstanding work. However, half an hour before the fundraiser, he sheepishly informed her that there was a last-minute change of plan. The next day she would learn that another Liberal woman councillor had been nominated by him to be elevated to the House of Lords. He explained that he needed someone to understand Britain's housing problem. Zerbanoo remembers telling Ashdown that she too was an elected councillor and knew a great deal about housing as she had been the London organizer for Shelter, the housing charity. She also knew all the ethnic minority communities, their needs and aspirations and they too needed representation. It was then that it hit her that so much of what Ashdown said and did was just bluff.

An Asian donor felt that the Asian communities were rich milch cows for the shrewd politician.

We were the cash machine in the wall that just gave pound notes and never even received a 'thank you'. I remember being invited to a garden party organized to get money off rich Asians. Zerbanoo was away on a speaking engagement abroad. We were all anxious that she should be given a half-winnable parliamentary seat to speak on behalf of the community that trusted and admired her. We asked Ashdown what he was doing about it. If we supported him with our wealth and votes would he support at least one of us to get elected to Parliament? Ashdown replied roughly that Asians needed to go through the system and first become elected councillors and hold office in the party and only then try for a parliamentary seat. We all realized then that Ashdown was a joker. Zerbanoo had not only made history being elected into office but she had also served on and chaired so many committees for the Liberals and had already fought two unwinnable parliamentary seats with an extraordinary high vote. She used to represent the Liberals on the media and was seen as the face of ethnic minorities in the Liberal party. We all knew then that the Liberal Democrats were no different from any other British political party and Zerbanoo was wasting her time with them.

In 2007, after the successful launch of Zerbanoo's book, *Confessions to a Serial Womaniser*, a high-powered committee was set up to collect over 400 letters from the good and great from across the globe to send to the cabinet office requesting the then prime minister to give Zerbanoo the honour that her country should have given her nearly a generation ago. The letters, which were from not only the highest placed women in the United Nations, the Commonwealth and the Iraqi parliament, but also international charities and prominent individuals whose work Zerbanoo impacted, make fascinating reading. As historical memoranda, they clearly reflect that her tireless work for others has been recognized the world over, but not in her own country.

In 2010, the then prime minister, Gordon Brown, suggested Zerbanoo's name for an MBE. Zerbanoo thought it was inappropriate to accept it. A member of the cabinet office appointment team did telephone and ask why she had politely turned it down. Zerbanoo informed the civil servant that taking up the honour would be disrespectful to those distinguished individuals and organizations that had nominated her. He responded that he had never heard of any Asian turning anything down. To which Zerbanoo retorted saying that now he had come across one. The conversation ended there.

Interestingly, Zerbanoo's hero, the first Asian Member of Parliament, Dadabhai Naoroji, never received any British honours. Today, he is revered as the Grand Old Man of India. In contrast, the second Asian Member of Parliament quickly took a knighthood from Lord Salisbury, the same Conservative prime minister who, before the general election of 1892, had said no one in Britain would vote for a black man, meaning Naoroji. His statement outraged Queen Victoria. Lord Salisbury had to eat his words when Dadabhai Naoroji was elected. When the Conservative Asian, Mancherjee Bhownagree, was elected to parliament a few years later in 1895, Lord Salisbury first gave him a knighthood and then wickedly nicknamed him Sir Bow and Agree.

Zerbanoo never kowtowed to anyone. The political issues she championed were as diverse as her constituents. Throughout her political career she has concentrated on improving the lives of others, whether it was to push for an allowance to be paid to those who worked at home caring for the young, old and those with disabilities, or speeding up the process to change the century-old underground drainage system that had choked and collapsed in her constituency.

Zerbanoo also pressed for the inclusion of eastern languages in schools. Although most politicians, in the early eighties, had not envisaged that countries like India and China would, years later, catapult into positions of power, she had the foresight to know that the world would someday recognize their untapped potential. She was quoted saying to the media as early as 1982:

The countries of the future are Asia and the Far East.

In England, there is a population who can already speak many foreign languages. Britain is a trading nation and can therefore reap tremendous advantage by speaking the language of the country she is trading with. There is a group of British people who have these talents and they are not being used. It is as important today to speak Hindi, Urdu or Mandarin as it is to speak French or German.

Considering the expanding ethnic minority population that were vegetarian, Zerbanoo made it a point to campaign for provision of vegetarian meals for the elderly at home and in hospitals. The diverse issues she juggled with stretched from availability of homeopathy medicine, to yoga being included as part of the curriculum in schools, to British Sikhs being allowed to wear the holy turban whilst working on construction sites. There were other cases that literally raised a stink. On one occasion, when excrement was being put through doors of blind people's homes by sadistic yobs amused by the distress they caused, Zerbanoo alerted the police to take action. She also campaigned for the young tearaways to have a centre to go to in the evenings to entertain themselves in a more constructive way.

In the early eighties, the members of the Hare Krishna Temple were deeply concerned that the government was threatening to close down their temple in Letchmore Heath because of the lack of parking spaces. Zerbanoo took up the fight on behalf of Hindu worshippers by pointing out that Westminster Abbey and many synagogues had no parking spaces either, but were not closed down. Why was a Hindu shrine being singled out? Letters were fired off and articles written by her demanding why permission was granted for a large cash-and-carry (a temple of consumerism) in the area and yet a 'temple of worship' was to be closed down.

It was her propensity for philanthropy that had her packing in eighty hours a week, working without a break. Her old diary gives a glimpse of her super-packed schedule. The time-intensive itinerary reads:

- Launching a national appeal for education for blacks in apartheid South Africa with the Archbishop of Canterbury at Lambeth Palace;
- Speaking to students at Oxford University;
- Talking to farmers in Radlett about food subsidies; and
- Attending a meeting of the Liberal Democrats Federal Executives.

The Liberal Democrats Federal Executives was the party's governing body into which she had just been elected. Zerbanoo was the first non-white in Britain elected into the board of any British political party. The same night, she was going out on the streets of Borehamwood, in Hertfordshire, canvassing for the elections she was determined to win.

Eager to cover more ground than most of her worn-out opponents during the parliamentary elections, Zerbanoo did the rounds of pubs, betting shops, supermarkets, churches, women's groups, schools and local associations, shaking thousands of hands all along the way. Constantly on the move, thinking of innovative ideas on how to reach out to a vast cross-section of society, she strategized by sending letters in the regional Indian languages of Gujarati and Urdu to some of her constituents

who were not fluent in English. A couple of volunteers readily
translated her mission statement into the regional languages that
spoke directly to the ethnic minority voters. The Tory party got
wind of it. Not wanting to be left out, they too sent letters in
Gujarati to everyone with foreign names including Sri Lankans,
Bengalis and Africans. The copycat campaign backfired badly
and ended up offending more people than it pleased.

In the roller-coaster ride of life there were as many downs as
ups. Zerbanoo would like to forget the time she spearheaded a
charity dinner to celebrate fifty years of Indian Independence.
The main draw for the event was to be Prince Charles, someone
Zerbanoo respects for his dedication to empowering the young
and being a committed environmentalist. The grand event had
been arranged down to the last detail. Fifty major charities
with branches in India would attend the function at the famous
Harrow School. The celebration was a brilliant way for the
rich and sought-after Indian community in Britain to meet
diverse leaders from the charity sector involved with important
groundbreaking work in India and Britain.

Zerbanoo set about making lavish arrangements for this
dinner. She believed that when the right people are offered
an opportunity to meet one another, wonderful things could
happen for the less fortunate.

At that time, Zerbanoo had also written a book for the
Channel 4 educational television series *Celebrating India*. It was to
tie in with the fiftieth anniversary of Indian Independence. The
book was well received in schools, as was the TV programme.

Then, a few weeks before the much anticipated dinner, there
was a letter from Prince Charles's office stating he was unable
to accept the invite as he had accepted another invitation to

the Albert Hall and was only able to attend one function to celebrate India's golden jubilee celebration.

It was devastating news after so much effort, time and resources had been invested in the event. Zerbanoo remembers, 'I was in India finalizing everything for so many other organizations although I had no staff and was not being paid for my work. I felt rather deflated and didn't know what to do.'

Zerbanoo was in Mumbai with her industrialist friend and mentor Sohrab Godrej, at the time. He tried to give her the moral support she needed.

Sohrab just said, 'I am so sorry. Please don't worry, as life plays funny tricks on us. I think my dear friend, the Queen Mother, would be upset at what has happened.'

I still remember his trusted and kind assistant, Rumi Majoo, cheering me up with my favourite drink of watermelon juice.

I had bought a box set of videos of the BBC series *I, Claudius* – the brilliant portrayal of the Roman Emperors and their machinations. Sohrab and I sat down and watched it together to take my mind off things. I think that evening I decided that I really did not mind paying the BBC licence fee if they produced such outstanding drama. I also realized how unpredictable and wicked life can be. The next day I flew back home to London. The other members of the events committee suggested we cancel the dinner even though so much work had gone into it. They thought the opportunity for charities to meet wealthy donors had been lost.

When most of the affluent Indian attendees heard that Prince Charles was going to another event, they started opting out.

Finally, we had to cancel the evening. It seemed, at the time, that I had wasted an entire year of my life. Although so much good could have come from that function, I knew it was not meant to be. I suppose we propose and God disposes. Maybe the time wasn't right, who knows. What is important is the good intention and the hard grind to make it happen. Everything else is not of our making. In the Hindu religious text, the Bhagavad Gita, it is put so beautifully, 'Your right is to action alone, not to its fruits at any time, never should they move you to act, or be attached to inaction.'

It took three more months to tie up the loose ends that the cancellation of the event had caused. Zerbanoo made it a point to personally visit every individual charity and apologize to all those who had readily donated money. Most people genuinely appreciated the effort, considering she could have easily posted a letter of apology along with a cheque.

The public embarrassment was handled with dignity and integrity. A couple of years later, she was busy again organizing a fundraiser for Prince Charles. As a member of the Advisory Committee and then vice chair of the Prince's Community Business Trust, Zerbanoo, along with the other committee members, proposed a dinner at Kensington Palace to be hosted by two princes, Prince Charles and the Aga Khan. After months of dedicated work and planning, an exclusive, star-studded event was unveiled.

The invitees were men known for their extraordinary wealth. On the evening of the stellar event, Zerbanoo's husband, Richard, was rudely stopped at the palace gates and told by Lord Boardman, who held a position in the Prince's Trust that his invitation was not valid. Embarrassed by the rude interlude, Zerbanoo decided that she could not attend the event without Richard.

However, after some negotiating, Richard's official invite was accepted but Zerbanoo was curtly informed by Lord Boardman that she would not be seated at the top table as major donors had to be seated near the two princes. Zerbanoo responded by saying, 'Wherever I sit, every man in the room will notice me, so it was of no concern to me where I am seated.'

To Lord Boardman's annoyance, Prince Charles made a special detour when leaving the dinner to personally thank Zerbanoo for her work. During the dinner, Richard had told the Prince's equerry what had transpired. He in turn ensured that Prince Charles got to know of Zerbanoo's contribution and congratulated her for making the evening a memorable one.

Some months later, Zerbanoo attended a private gathering at Prince Charles's home in Highgrove, Gloucestershire, which she remembers with great fondness: 'As they say, third time lucky!'

In February 2001, Zerbanoo and Richard were invited to a very select gathering at Somerset House for the tenth anniversary of the 'Press Complaints Commission'. It was the first time Prince Charles and the Duchess of Cornwall, then still Camilla Parker Bowles, were seen together with Prince William. The royals as well as Richard and Zerbanoo rubbed shoulders with George Michael (a client of Richard's firm), Spice Girl Geri Halliwell, soap stars, senior politicians and most of the editors of national newspapers.

During this period, Zerbanoo had realized that party politics was not for her. A chain of events had made her reassess her life and seriously question whether politics was her true vocation.

British broadcaster and journalist Jeremy Paxman, writes in his book *The Political Animal: An Anatomy*, 'Politicians: they are either untrustworthy, power hungry, hypocritical misfits or hopeless idealists doomed to languish forever on the backbenches.'

Coincidentally, Jeremy and Zerbanoo share the same birthday and year of birth, as well as similar views on the political scene. Jeremy writes that politics is a tough, unforgiving business.

> Those political careers that don't end in defeat or disgrace frequently disappear into obscurity. It can take years to move from activist to counsellor, and then if you are very lucky, to MP. And what sort of person likes having their business or family life splashed all over the news? Or their mistakes trumpeted and their triumphs belittled?

What was it that made Zerbanoo want to swim with the sharks in the cesspool of politics? Why was she attracted to such a tough, unforgiving and an uncertain business? Did it satisfy a deep-rooted psychological need within her? Even she cannot answer that question.

Zerbanoo stood for Parliament three times, in 1983, 1987 and 1992 as a Liberal Democrat, a political party not known for winning elections. It makes one wonder why she continued to fight elections if there was little hope of winning and so much unpleasantness.

There is no doubting that she got a serious buzz out of being in the forefront of making things happen. She got a definite high but, more than that, it gave her 'A deep sense of purpose and meaning'. Politics was for Zerbanoo a means of channelling her passion for justice.

One of the people who acknowledges Zerbanoo's role is the Afro-American Jerome Mack, a key player in diversity and equality training. Jerome was an esteemed adviser to numerous British government bodies and many major companies. He recalls several occasions when Zerbanoo made significant contributions to his efforts to assist the British Police in improving their service delivery to ethnic minority communities.

On one particular occasion, I'd held a strategic planning session on improving race relations in London for the Metropolitan Police Commissioner and his staff. Zerbanoo was one of the guest speakers whom I had invited to share their experiences of policing in London. She narrated a series of personal anecdotes that helped participants to understand the importance of mutual respect in police/public encounters. Zerbanoo spoke with such sincerity and humanity that she was able to connect with all those who attended the event. An assistant commissioner called me to the side before his departure and told me that Zerbanoo's presentation had caused him to reflect on his own past behaviour as a beat officer. He spoke of his intention to take every opportunity to ensure his officers were aware of the need for courtesy and respect when engaging with ethnic minority citizens.

A leading light in the British Chinese community, Thomas Chan, former Conservative Mayor and the Queen's Deputy Lieutenant of Greater London, calls Zerbanoo, '智者', Chinese for 'the wise one'. His first encounter with Zerbanoo was in

1998 when both were invited by the then home secretary, the
Rt. Hon. Jack Straw MP, to serve on his newly established Race
Relations Forum.

> There was a sense of serenity about Zerbanoo as she
> descended into the Home Office boardroom, which by then
> was full of anticipation. Most members were from the who's
> who in the race relations industry. I remember Zerbanoo's
> arrival was greeted by everyone with a sense of 'rejoice'.
> I do not know until today whether they were glad to hear
> her words of wisdom or because they realized they were in
> excellent company.
>
> She stood out as someone of immense intellect, clarity
> of mind and purpose, yet she was also outwardly cultured
> and courteous. Even during this very first encounter, I was
> able to observe through her contributions that she meant
> business. To me, she is a walking oracle. She can read people
> instinctively. Although there were many distinguished people
> amongst the members of the Forum, somehow Zerbanoo
> was able to use her power of observation to discern the good
> from the indifferent amongst us all.

Calling her a 'neatly-packaged stick of dynamite that needs
handling with care and respect', he says he is lucky that their
stars met when they did.

> As a result of this encounter, I was able to be involved with
> the work of ASHA and we have since become firm friends.
> Zerbanoo loves everything Chinese and her exquisite Chinese
> embroideries must rival that of any Empress. If there is one

woman who could be firm friends with Confucius, it would be Zerbanoo. Despite his traditional ideology about women's role in society, Zerbanoo would outwit him with her charm and diplomacy. She is someone who might even persuade the great man to amend his analects and give women the position in society that they so rightly deserve.

Zerbanoo's work with women and children came in many shapes and forms. The West Harrow Park was once a part of her constituency, and a haven for drug-pushers and shady characters. The park had a murky pond that would fill up with slush each time it rained and was a junkyard awash with broken bottles, old bicycles, condoms, you name it.

A request was put in to the council to clean it up but Zerbanoo was given the blanket answer that no funds were available to clear up the mess. A week later, there was a frantic call from the principal of a local school informing her that a schoolboy, Darrell McNally, was in hospital after suffering a horrific stomach injury. He had fallen into the pond and slashed his intestines on shards of broken glass. Ironically, it was just a few days prior to the incident that Zerbanoo had drawn the council's attention to the dismal state of the pond overflowing with rubbish. Furious with the lackadaisical attitude of the council, Zerbanoo threatened to personally sue them as a citizen if they did not take action.

In the aftermath of the incident, one of the first things Zerbanoo did was organize the local community into a Parks' Committee. Darrell McNally's injury had garnered a sense of collective support from the community. Trees were planted and the local students helped design a children's play area. In the wake of the public outcry, Zerbanoo was quick to tie in all the threads of community support and a popular summer play scheme was introduced for children whose mothers had to work during their holidays.

The same park, which had served as a short cut to the West Harrow station, had poor lighting. It posed a problem for women who returned late from work and walked through the park to make their way home on the other side. When Zerbanoo brought it to the council's attention, the jaded councillors ridiculed her. It evoked crude remarks, 'Oh, Mrs Gifford wants lights in the park so that it will be easier for men to see what the women look like.'

The following week a woman was raped in the park, followed by another unfortunate incident. The residents were outraged by the apathy of the council members. The Mayor had no option but to issue a public apology. Zerbanoo remembers that,

> The men had to eat their words and install the lights. It took an ugly incident for the council to do their job, which they should have done in the first place. It was the short-sightedness of politicians and the crudeness which angered me. They had little concern for women or the expense that came from violence against women and children. Nor did they want to acknowledge that one rape involves police time, court time, social services time and, worst of all, the horror that a woman suffers that no time will heal.
>
> These days when you switch on the television there are daily news bulletins about well-known public figures being exposed as rapists and paedophiles. It is a sign of our times that people now have the courage to bravely expose the

underbelly of those in power and highlight the violence and humiliation women and children have been subjected to. Women have been treated atrociously because we have had no voice, and those few who did speak out were accused of being harpies. It was very different a generation ago for those of us campaigning to stop this vileness. It was embarrassing for me as a young mother to address such issues in a room full of uncaring men. I felt humiliated.

Encouraging women to have the confidence to stand for posts, expanding the pool of female leadership talent and helping other women win elections are achievements of which Zerbanoo is proud. Her pioneering work in facilitating better provisions for working mothers is the one closest to her heart.

Sue Stapely, former head of PR at the Law Society and today a strategic communications consultant stands testimony for it.

I have known and worked with Zerbanoo since the eighties when we both became involved in politics. We were soon collaborating. I had been working at the BBC then, busy building my career. Zerbanoo had already become active in politics as a councillor but we came together when I helped set up the 300 Group. I was the first chair of the 300 Group, which was set up to bring more women into political and public life. Zerbanoo was a rare thing, an active, committed and vocal member, an Asian woman prepared to put her nose above the parapet. We watched in admiration as she battled her way up the political ladder and I remain amazed that she is not in one or the other of the Houses of Parliament today. The Liberals have missed a trick and are the poorer as a result.

Providing the sepia-toned backdrop of the eighties, when they both stood for general elections, Sue retraces the course of events without airbrushing her words.

Zerbanoo stood for the Liberals and I for the Social Democratic Party, which I had helped set up. I chaired the Women for Social Democracy and we collaborated when the two parties formed the Alliance and agreed to fight the election on a shared basis. Few of us were successful, though many of us secured high votes and support. The voters simply lacked the courage to do something different, as most of them do to this day. The climate was tough for women trying to make their way in the political world. The House of Commons operated to suit men, and the few women who achieved high office either came from political dynasties, were child-free or, like Margaret Thatcher, had high-earning husbands prepared to bankroll their childcare and domestic lives.

Most women were forced to play the men's game but many were not prepared to. Those of us sometimes described as superwomen who managed to juggle careers, children, marriages and the time-consuming life and expense of political ambition, were often difficult colleagues for the men, who had all but the last aspect of their lives taken care of by others. Having failed to secure winnable seats, many of us then abandoned the political world with its awful hours, poor rewards, endless backbiting and manoeuvring, and returned to make successes of our careers. But Zerbanoo battled on, fighting for women, here and abroad, and continues to do so to this day.

Journalist Tim Symonds sees Zerbanoo as a brilliant shooting star orbiting the political space. He says, 'Zerbanoo, to observers of contemporary British politics, was like Haley's Comet to the astronomer. Like Haley's Comet, political activists with her energy, flair and sheer chutzpah only come along every seventy-five years.'

EIGHT

BUFFALO BILL

Zerbanoo's feminist friend, lawyer Baroness Helena Kennedy QC (Queen's Counsel), had once described the equal representation of women in politics as waiting for fish to grow feet. Both Zerbanoo and Helena had been at the forefront of campaigns to empower women through the political and legal systems still dominated by men in the eighties. The feisty women were guest speakers at the NAWO (National Alliance of Women Organisations) annual conference and later spoke at St. Martin-in-the-Fields on the issue of 'Justice' They continued to fight for equal representation for women in public life.

At the time, Zerbanoo was quoted as saying: 'England is a no-women's land.' Addressing the guests at the launch of the All Party Women's Lobby to promote women's interests through the parliamentary system, Zerbanoo passionately declared, 'Women are not so much the second sex as the forgotten sex. But, they will be forgotten no longer. We have heard fine words from various politicians and party leaders, now we need fine actions.'

Publicly urging more women to take an active part and stand for parliament and public office, she drummed the message, 'Nothing happens by itself. It only happens when people make it happen.'

Coaxing women to take the power into their hands, she tried to instil in them a sense of purpose to step out of the kitchen and into public life. In her words: 'It is up to women to see that they are properly represented at every level of society. For far too long women have been short-changed by successive governments, anxious for their votes but unwilling to address their special needs.'

The sustained campaign to realign the balance of men and women in parliament continued in her public speeches and in her regular newspaper columns. In 1986, she wrote in an article in *Midweek* titled 'MPs on Tap at Kitchen Sink': 'At the moment, Parliament is full of middle-aged, middle-class men and that's not democracy. There are 32 women out of 635 MPs and that means the potential of half the population is wasted.'

Dismayed by the negative attitude towards women in the early eighties, she became a vociferous member of the newly formed 300 Group. Spearheaded by Lesley Abdela, the distinguished international expert on women's rights, the 300 Group relentlessly lobbied for equal representation of women in national and European politics.

The 300 Group took the initiative of grooming young girls for public life. They were determined to break the constant stalemate as far as women were concerned. The cost of hiring a venue was substantially reduced when Zerbanoo offered to host a series of seminars at her home. The workshops encouraged young women to seek and hold public office by providing comprehensive training on skills required to become elected councillors, MPs and Members of the European Parliament. The aspiring politicians were groomed in the art of public-speaking, campaigning and leadership skills. They shadowed Zerbanoo as she campaigned and interacted with the national media, giving them a real feel of the life of a politician.

All those involved in the political leadership training programme firmly believed that the feminization of politics would lead to a better and more sustainable world. Unlike some, Zerbanoo was not apologetic about being a woman. On the contrary, she thought being a woman gave her a distinct edge.

> I take great pride in the fact that women are complex, creative and the centre of the community. We have an emotional GPS, an unspoken intelligence that we are attuned to. Women are intuitive, can multitask and are able to mix emotions with reason. We are more conciliatory, are lateral thinkers and make sure we get the end result. 'The rooster may crow but it is the hen that lays the eggs.' Women are the doers. In the past, many women struggled hard to be recognized and many were made to sacrifice their femininity and family life.

Confident of her innate feminine power and the ability to deliver what was expected of her, she never felt the need to be an honorary man. Even whilst entering a strictly boys' club, she particularly enjoyed being herself, challenging stereotypes every step of the way.

Using her soft power and platform to make a societal change, she shared her personal story.

Young mothers who enter political life are accused of maternal deprivation regardless of the actual quality of the relationship they may have with their children. For those blinkered people I shall always be difficult to accept. However, my visibility has also been a source of encouragement for many. No modern democracy can afford to be so lopsided and terrified of the 'Shakti', the goddess of creation, change and liberation. The world can't afford to dismiss the female principle which brings balance and creativity.

Dr Kusoom Vadgama, an Indo-British historian, has watched a battle-scarred Zerbanoo fight for women's rights ever since she first spotted her on television while channel-surfing. Impressed as she listened to an Indian speak with such conviction, she's followed Zerbanoo's career as a game changer. Dr Vadgama feels that, 'Zerbanoo's rock-solid foundation of Eastern philosophy, cushioned by Western enterprise, gave her a balanced approach and a rare insight on power play.'

Zerbanoo was at the heart of the women's empowerment movement at a time when women had meekly internalized their role as societal scapegoats. She was able to explain with empathy that, 'Caged birds don't sing, they cry.'

Everyone needs freedom. Zerbanoo had this extraordinary need to open all the cages that trapped vulnerable women.

Working across a spectrum of pressing issues concerning women, she reached out to a cross-section of women across the globe. Former Jamaican diplomat, Patsy Robertson, first met Zerbanoo at a public gathering. The two kept in touch as their paths subsequently crossed at high-powered meetings. Patsy was, for a generation, the official spokesperson for the Commonwealth and later a UN senior media adviser on women. She had an opportunity to see first-hand the change that Zerbanoo was trying to initiate.

Zerbanoo has always supported my international work with widows. You don't have to explain to Zerbanoo the importance of empowering women; she only wants to know how she can help. She has been an enthusiastic support for action to eradicate racism, religious intolerance, social exclusion to name a few of the issues which still dominate much of the world's discourse. I have worked closely with her in establishing the ASHA Centre where her dream of bringing together people from all races, religions and nationalities in a beautiful and serene setting to discuss and work their way through long held prejudices and hatred, has been a triumphant success.

Unlike today, when the media is open about exposing domestic violence and publicly shaming the perpetrators, in the early eighties the subject was still taboo. Whenever Zerbanoo tried to raise the horrors of violence against vulnerable women and children, she was briskly told off. Ironically, it was other influential women who told her, in no uncertain terms, that discussing rape, domestic violence and child abuse was unhelpful. No one in their right mind spoke publicly about such unladylike issues. Those involved were meant to sort it out themselves without interference from the police or politicians. When Zerbanoo failed to toe the line, she received a letter stating that her political career could be short-lived if she continued to champion the need to change the way those in authority approached violence against women and children.

Ignoring these warnings, Zerbanoo continued to support those silenced by society. Underlying her zeal for social justice there was an unfulfilled fate that was larger than politics. Every stumbling block worked as a trigger for her to help people with acts of kindness. Evidence of this can be seen in her archives that overflow with touching tributes from people living as far away as Russia and Columbia, to Pakistan, Arabia, Africa, Japan and Mongolia.

The letters came from political and media figures, and organizations all over the world. A letter from an Iraqi member of parliament, Zakia Hakki, the first woman judge in the Middle East, goes as far as to say that Zerbanoo should be given a Nobel Peace Prize for the work she had done for women internationally. The common theme that runs through them is the selflessness with which Zerbanoo worked, devoting her time, unconditional friendship and dedication to their cause.

Ina Gjikondi first contacted Zerbanoo when she was Chair of the Albanian United Nations Association. Upon spotting Zerbanoo's website for inspirational women, in 2006, Ina's interest was piqued by the international mentoring scheme being offered. She got in touch, thereby starting a long-lasting friendship. Years later, Zerbanoo invited Ina to attend the Z-Factor exhibition held in May 2012 at the Women's Library in London. The exhibition celebrated thirty years of Zerbanoo being in public life.

Ina remembers the big day of the Z-Factor exhibition.

When Zerbanoo spoke, she owned the stage and used humour to interact with the audience. She does not speak with a script, but she does her homework. The discipline and flexibility are two things that she has married together wonderfully in her public-speaking skills. She connects with the heart.

The next day, after the exhibition, as we walked in the hallways in the House of Lords, the one place I wanted to visit, I remember to our surprise, at the very moment we sat down, there was a personal tribute paid to Zerbanoo. Baroness Royall, the Leader of the House of Lords, singled out Zerbanoo Gifford as a tireless campaigner for justice and human rights and a passionate advocate for democracy and women's empowerment. It was amazing considering no one knew this was going to happen. Zerbanoo was just there in the right place at the right time. The next evening, Zerbanoo took me to a VIP reception at the Mayfair home of the philanthropist Meera Gandhi. I wanted to meet Cherie Blair who was to be there. Zerbanoo cut through the gathering and went straight to her. Cherie recognized Zerbanoo since she had meet her at the celebrity reception at No 10 Downing Street to celebrate Tony Blair's landslide victory in 1997.

On her visit to Albania in 2014, I introduced her to the deputy prime minister, Niko Peleshi, to discuss how she could help empower young Albanians on the lines of the work she is doing at the ASHA Centre in England. She was then invited to attend the historic reopening of the nuclear bunker built during the communist regime in the seventies. There she met the new socialist prime minister, Edi Rama.

There is no doubt that there will be an ASHA Centre in Albania in the near future as she has the vision to see the possibilities that other people overlook or are afraid of approaching.

Zerbanoo makes things happen every day with the speed of light as she drives herself and others to action. She inspired me to co-create a women's inspirational website called Women Inspire Action in Washington DC, where I now work around the issues of leadership and women. Zerbanoo's photograph was up at the Women's Museum in Washington DC when America celebrated ninety years of woman's suffrage. She's been a role model for us.

The Lila Fellows also see Zerbanoo as their role model. The Lila Foundation is the brainchild of Lila Poonawalla, former managing director of Alfa Laval India, who used her fiftieth birthday gift money from her former employer to fund an educational trust in India. The trust empowers young Indian girls from Pune by supporting academically outstanding and financially deserving students to pursue higher education. Lila joined hands with Zerbanoo in an extraordinary experiment that involved flying the young girls to England. The underprivileged girls known to excel academically had never travelled overseas before or even owned an overcoat. It was an opportunity of a lifetime made possible by two remarkable women.

Talking of the memorable time when Zerbanoo first suggested a joint leadership programme, Lila admits that she was apprehensive knowing it would cost an arm and a leg. She fondly recollects:

But Zerbanoo put my concern to rest. She announced a programme of three weeks for my girls, fourteen in number to be selected by me. Zerbanoo would provide free board and training and I would take care of air travel and other personal expenses. We started in 2009 and since then five batches of fourteen girls each have gone through this amazing programme. The girls had a chance to experience some of Britain's best talent and be trained by them in communication and leadership skills as well as corporate and personal development. It's been a dream come true for them as they were also able to visit London, Stratford-upon-Avon, Bath, Oxford and the beautiful Welsh countryside. The results were outstanding.

International development guru, Lena Choudary-Salter gives Zerbanoo credit for creating a circle of connectivity.

For those of us in the field of development she understands the interconnectedness of issues and the need for lasting and fruitful partnerships across organizations. I shall never forget an occasion when she was addressing a high-powered audience. She wove my work on water shortage and women's sexual reproduction into her speech. She called me remarkable. For the past twenty years I have felt obliged to be remarkable. Zerbanoo makes us connect with our own power and purpose in such a big-hearted way.

Ruth Powys vouches for it. CEO of Elephant Family, a charity founded by Mark Shand, the brother of the Duchess of

Cornwall and Prince Charles's brother-in-law, Ruth expounds on Zerbanoo's sense of resourcefulness saying Zerbanoo's infectiously positive approach to solving issues has had a major impact on the work of so many charities and me personally.

Over the years she spent a significant amount of time with the Elephant Family's approach to reaching the Asian community and enabling us to raise substantial funds for the conservation of endangered Asian elephants.

When Ruth initially approached Zerbanoo for help with fundraising, she was in for a surprise. Before Ruth knew what was happening, the two of them were on a night train in India, travelling from Delhi to Dehradun. The ease with which it all transpired augured what was to come next. As the train rattled into the darkness of the night, Ruth discovered that they were sharing a serendipitous moment with BBC's Mark Tully, a fellow traveller on the same train. Ruth, a fan of the BBC's celebrity anchor, secretly wondered if Zerbanoo had prearranged it. While meeting Mark Tully in the initial part of their journey was coincidental, the moment certainly bookmarked the beginning of the great Indian adventure.

Upon arriving at the remote village, home to the tribal Gujjar community, Ruth and Zerbanoo were escorted to a specially built stage. The village was rife with rumours that the gori memsahibs (fair ladies) had arrived from vilayat (foreign lands) and were going to donate money. They were the cynosure of all eyes.

Without bothering to deliver a speech that was expected of her, Zerbanoo got down to business. Noticing that it was a strictly male gathering, she wanted to know why there were no women present. The men justified the women's absence by declaring that they were the decision-makers *not* the women.

Zerbanoo wasn't ready to accept it. She sternly demanded that the women of the village step out of their homes. Her terse tone commanded attention. The men didn't have a choice but to comply. Gradually the wives, daughters and sisters shuffled into the dilapidated community hall. The men cut a sorry figure as they anxiously peered through the open doors and windows in an attempt to catch snatches of the conversation. They were curious to know what was transpiring between the foreign ladies and their women folk.

Zerbanoo issued precise instructions for the doors and windows to be bolted from the inside. The men were bluntly told to leave the premises. Addressing the women who were rarely given any importance, she asked them to come forward with their problems. She quietly listened and suggested long-term solutions.

As soon as she had won their confidence, some of the women opened up saying they didn't want a sewing machine like everyone thought they required. They just weren't interested in sewing. Instead, it was the lack of healthcare facilities that was their cause for concern. They unanimously agreed that a mobile health clinic to visit the village on a regular basis would be of great help.

After a great deal of discussion, the women came to a consensus that they would like to own a buffalo each to help them sustain their livelihood. The moment the decision was made, Zerbanoo spontaneously whisked out a generous donation from her own pocket. It was to buy the first buffalo that she named Buffalo Bill, much to Ruth's amusement. It was seed money for the women to start with. She later followed it up with a substantial donation.

This was an auspicious beginning to the empowering of rural women marginalized by the society. The arrangement effectively changed the power structure in the village as the women were gifted an opportunity to become the breadwinners of their families. They found a voice and had real economic power invested in them. The simple act of empowering them was the first step in their long journey towards becoming the decision-makers of their community.

Talking about shifting the balance of power, Zerbanoo dissects it with her trademark humour:

> If you control the wealth in a community, you have power. People talk about equality and have conferences until the 'buffaloes' come home. But, if you want to make a difference you have to go out there and take the 'buffalo' by its horns. It's about changing the way we operate. Up until then, the women had been intimidated into giving the power to the men. The head man of the village actually had a stick in his hand and was hitting the women on the back of their legs, shoving them along in the same way that one would corral animals into a pen. He saw that I was furious and had the sense to stop.

Certain organizations inadvertently make those they are helping more dependent on them rather than less. It is wonderful to be a provider, but it is more important to ensure that those you are helping can stand on their own two feet. Quoting the parable in the Bible she says: 'When Jesus says, 'rise up and take thy bed and walk,' Jesus didn't carry the bed for the man. He gave him the power and confidence to heal himself by becoming self-motivated and self-sufficient. This is the miracle.'

During their stay in India, Zerbanoo and Ruth were invited to spend time with the founder of Stree Shakti – The Parallel Force and Global Women Forum – Rekha Mody, at her beautiful Kolkata home. It was an opportunity for them to visit the centre that the development activist had funded for disadvantaged women and their children. They witnessed first-hand, women being empowered, financially and spiritually, by teaching them the forgotten arts and crafts of India while their children attended the adjoining school.

While in Kolkata, Zerbanoo stayed at Rekha's home, surrounded by exquisite works of art that she had commissioned from India's leading painters.

The highlight of her stay at the Mody residence was its spectacular art gallery effect.

Rekha had exhibited, in her spacious sitting room just for our stay a series of Mona Lisa paintings each created by a different Indian artist. I was overwhelmed with so many *Mona Lisa*s looking back at me. Especially the one dressed as a Maharani holding a lily in her hand. I had never seen anything like this anywhere in all my travels. I think even Leonardo daVinci would have approved of so many *Mona Lisa*s smiling enigmatically at each other as if to say we know we have taken your breath away by our collective beauty.

While in Delhi, Zerbanoo was invited to address the IV International Congress on Women, Work and Health with delegates from over twenty countries. Rekha recalls,

Zerbanoo enthralled the international audience by her speech at the inaugural session. She explained that we watch the same moon, breathe the same air and so were inevitably connected to each other and needed to change the world together. She challenged all present to make others learn more, do more and become more. She motivated everyone to become game changers. Having known Zerbanoo for over two decades, I admire her dedication to the cause of empowerment of women.

Zerbanoo was honoured in Los Angeles at the 'India Splendor' event organized by one of India's leading business tycoons, Dr Modi of Spice Global, an Indian conglomerate headquartered in Singapore. The only two women awarded were Zerbanoo and the actress, Aishwarya Rai Bachchan. Dr Modi says: 'They were both chosen for their different contributions to society. Both women are strong, independent, and inherently very beautiful.'

Acknowledging Zerbanoo's contributions to humanitarian causes, Modi believes her social work singles her out as a highly conscious, international citizen who connects with people at a level that goes beyond gender, nationality and religion.

He says, 'Zerbanoo has broken glass ceilings as a woman. She has underlined her primary identity as a global citizen, strongly aware of issues affecting the world as she in her own unique way tries to remedy some problems that affect the world today.'

A global citizen himself, Dr Modi believes that the ASHA foundation founded by Zerbanoo connects very closely with the objectives of Global Citizen Forum, an NGO he initiated to unite citizens, thinkers and social pioneers to create a better world order.

Even whilst she was being celebrated, Zerbanoo never stopped raising a toast to the outstanding achievements of women in every field. *Confessions to a Serial Womaniser: Secrets of the World's Inspirational Women,* her latest book, is an ode to incredible women who have transformed their own lives and that of others through dint of their hard work, guts and acts of compassion. Interviewing over 300 prominent women across sixty countries for the book was a tough job, but one that Zerbanoo cherished.

Confessions to a Serial Womaniser was conceived out of the NESTA fellowship (the National Endowment for Science, Technology and the Arts) that Zerbanoo was awarded. This fellowship programme operates through talent-spotting rather than open application. Zerbanoo's fellowship facilitated the collection of remarkable stories of inspirational women around the world.

The book launch, in central London at the National Portrait Gallery in 2007, had a press report saying:

The place was heaving with international celebrities. The

Duchess of York and Britain's first woman foreign secretary, Margaret Beckett, rubbed shoulders with Oscar-winning actresses, ambassadors and the world's media. The three-year NESTA project had Zerbanoo blurring timelines as she crisscrossed the globe in search of an esoteric hugging saint, a French Resistance heroine who took on the Gestapo, a spiritual giantess who danced with Fred Astaire and a high-flyer who was educated by an elephant, apart from 296 other inspiring women who courted fame and success. The diverse women warmed up to a variety of subjects that oscillated from pillow talk to advancement at the workplace and creating legacies.

One of Britain's senior professionals in the field of arts and culture, Venu Dhupa, started actively interacting with Zerbanoo when she was nominated to the NESTA Fellowship Programme. The programme was championed by Lord Puttnam of Queensgate, the Oscar-winning producer of the film *Chariots of Fire*, as a public endowment to encourage invention, innovation and exceptional talent. Venu states:

The book Zerbanoo wrote during her fellowship celebrated the work of women from all over the world with fantastic portraits commissioned by her and painted by Jeroo Roy. I was delighted to donate the framing of the major artwork via which transformed the tranquil halls of the National Portrait Gallery into the most vibrant opening I have ever experienced.

The book launch was combined with an unveiling of the artwork. I knew the investment from the public endowment would deliver value for money, but I had no idea how much value until years later, when I visited the ASHA Centre in the Forest of Dean to give a leadership workshop for bright young women from the Indian subcontinent. The impact of Zerbanoo's efforts has been immense and I am honoured to have been part of her journey.

Many women benefitted from the book *Confessions to a Serial Womaniser*. International conductor, Dr Sharon Choa, founder and artistic director of a new orchestra in East Anglia, states that the Chamber Orchestra Anglia has been given a tremendous boost as a result of Zerbanoo's book. 'I have been infinitely inspired by Zerbanoo to have the courage to forge ahead, to work as hard as one could, and to believe in one's vision.'

Sharon is now the head of music at the Hong Kong Academy of Performing Arts.

The outpouring of gratitude comes from all quarters and not just from renowned women. Ewa Piglowska, a Polish dress designer and seamstress, says Zerbanoo was her rock when she was going through a terrible phase in her life. Ewa was physically abused by her husband. Seeing her sorry plight, Zerbanoo was instrumental in helping her obtain legal help. Ewa made legal history by having her divorce become a test case decided by the judges in the House of Lords. She says, 'She was also there for me and my sons during my divorce and since then. For me, she is a prime example of solidarity between women who suffer at the hand of bullies.'

So many women spoke about a helping hand that quietly

reached out to them. Indu, a Dalit woman in Mumbai, blessed Zerbanoo for paying off her disabled son's hospital bills and revealed how Zerbanoo had marched off to a politician's office to ensure that her son was given a job in a telephone exchange. She says, 'She explained to the politician, who didn't want anything to do with disabled people, that being physically disabled did not mean being stupid. My son was given the job and is now the main provider for our family.'

Aili He, a Chinese doctor living in Britain, says her daughter Sally got an opportunity to do a postgraduate degree in music at the famous Cardiff International Academy of Voice, thanks to a scholarship organized by Zerbanoo.

I have no family in Britain. When my only daughter gave her final recital at the Royal Academy of Music, Mrs Gifford and her husband drove me to London and invited all their family and friends to attend the concert so that Sally would know she was supported. This encouraged Sally at a very tense time and she performed successfully. Very few people in Britain would think about a single, Chinese mother who needs friendship. When Sally was rehearsing for her auditions, she was encouraged by Mrs Gifford to sing to the builders at the ASHA Centre while they were working. They had never heard opera and were enchanted. Mrs Gifford has this idea that no talent should go unrecognized. Sally could have practised indoors with no audience. Instead, she sang to those that had never experienced classical music and their appreciation grew her confidence. This was a wonderful preparation for when Sally sang for the Pope.

In 1988, Zerbanoo became a hive of creative interaction, taking a year off to research and interview over a hundred successful Asian women living in Britain. The women of excellence found their voice in her well-received first book titled *The Golden Thread: Asian Experiences of Post-Raj Britain.*

The determination to give a platform to the Asian women came from a remark she took offence to on a television chat show in 1988. Benazir Bhutto had just been announced the prime minister of Pakistan. The TV guests present were mildly derogatory about Asian women, which annoyed Zerbanoo. She took the challenge on live television to research and write a book on the diversity of outstanding Asian women who had made Britain their home and to share their personal stories of successes and setbacks.

Shakira Caine, the Guiana-born model and wife of Michael Caine, was one of the women she met. Zerbanoo managed to interview Shakira at a time when she rarely gave interviews. They became good friends.

Later, when staunch feminist Gloria Steinem made a derogatory remark about Shakira Caine in a newspaper article, Zerbanoo wrote in Shakira's defence.

Actor Michael Caine was grateful for Zerbanoo's public support of his wife. He acknowledged the stand she took in his autobiography titled *What's It All About?*

He wrote in his bestselling book:

This new article made me see red because it not only attacked me, it attacked my wife Shakira. What Steinem actually wrote was, and I quote: 'Michael Caine is only attracted to subservient women and now he has found one.' This statement is not only completely uninformed but I found it the most offensive, patronising and condescending thing ever written about me and what is more important, an ignorant and hurtful criticism of my wife.

In her book, the *Golden Thread*, Zerbanoo Gifford wrote the following about Miss Steinem's statement:

Shakira has her own flourishing business and a happy marriage, despite living amid the lurid life of show business, accomplishments of which any person could be proud. To infer that she is a nameless doormat is hurtful as well as untrue, yet Shakira's reaction was simply to think how sad it was to think like that. So often it appears that women who claim to fight to liberate others become substitute authorities, judging by their own criteria the 'true role' of women. Shakira's choice to value her husband and daughter ahead of her own ambition was not a means by which to deny herself personal satisfaction, but one through which to gain it. The blind spots of certain Western feminists might make them unable to perceive that fulfilment can be gained through the giving of self as well as the promotion of self.

Sticking her neck out for issues she believes in comes as naturally as breathing to Zerbanoo.

NINE

A REAL HERO

Zerbanoo started to write because she felt 'the word' had the power to influence people's views. She hoped her writing would motivate people to go beyond self-limiting boundaries that come with the daily grind of living, and be inspired by the lives of others before them.

She believes that there are at least three ways to change people's mindsets. The first is by using legal measures to ensure change. The second is by writing and using powerful stories to inspire people. The third and the most important: to change oneself into a better person as an example of how change can truly come about.

Zerbanoo wished that people would take a page out of the life of Thomas Clarkson, the driving force behind the campaign to end the horrors of slavery. She thinks the selfless abolitionist who played a stellar role in the British and the American anti-slavery movement was not given the public acknowledgement he deserved. His invaluable contribution was pushed into obscurity.

Zerbanoo's first photograph

Zerbanoo breaking ranks, with her parents
Kitty and Bailey calling her back

Zerbanoo with her mother
Kitty in Pune

Family photograph with paternal great grandmother Zomord, grandfather Rustom and grandmother Gover sitting with aunty Hoshbanoo on her lap and Bailey in front of her

Zerbanoo and her father Bailey outside their London hotel

Zerbanoo's maternal great grandmother Gool in Iran

Family photograph with grandfather Shapoor Mazda sitting in the centre with his signature beard

Wedding day with Miss Pickering, Roedean School
friends and bridesmaids Pana and cousin Diane

Zerbanoo and Richard cutting their wedding cake in 1973

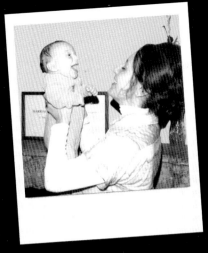

With her son Mark

Campaigning with
her son Alexander

Zerbanoo, Richard, Mark
and Alexander during 1983
General Election

Zerbanoo speaking at the
Liberal Democrat conference

Zerbanoo outside parliament with the
fashion students' competition winners

With Lord Steel at the House of
Commons for the launch of a Liberal
Commission chaired by Zerbanoo

Zerbanoo playing with the street
children cared for by the Snehasadan
home in Mumbai

Campaigning for better
Nursery facilities

Zerbanoo with Zinnia Khajotia and
Tricia Sibbons at the launch of her book
Asian Presence in Europe at the offices
of Anti-Slavery International

In the House of Commons for the launch of Dadabhai Naoroji Celebrations with the Maharana of Udaipur on the left and Sohrab Godrej on the right

Zerbanoo with Bishop Trevor Huddleston presenting 'The People's Petition' to 10 Downing Street calling for the release of Nelson Mandela

Receiving the Nehru Centenary Award from His Excellency Krishna Rasgotra

Receiving the Freedom of the City of Lincoln, Nebraska

Being blessed by Pope John Paul II at the Vatican in Rome

ASHA actors with Nelson Mandela at his home presenting their play on the history of modern South Africa to him

Delegates at the ASHA Centre having tea overlooked by the Jeroo Roy painting of 250 of the world's inspirational women

ASHA garden volunteers

Young Jewish and Palestinian actors breaking barriers at the ASHA Centre

'Our soul rocks at ASHA'

Zerbanoo and Richard
celebrating their pearl
anniversary in 2003

Zerbanoo with Alex
and Richard on Mark's
wedding to Monica

Zerbanoo's grandson
William Makepeace's
first day at Kindergarten

Zerbanoo with elder son Mark,
and Sandy and Lucie – members
of the ASHA team

the British people to call for the end of the slave trade as much as the cruelty inflicted on slaves who were transported to the West Indies and the Americas.

Zerbanoo wasn't aware of this guru of campaigning until she was asked to sit on the committee to commemorate the 150th death anniversary of Thomas Clarkson. A plaque was dedicated to Clarkson at Westminster Abbey, in September 1996. At long last, he could join the greats in British history commemorated there.

When the biography of the life of William Wilberforce, the British MP credited with initiating the law to abolish slavery, authored by his two sons was published in 1838 it caused an outrage. His sons had gone out of their way to ignore or belittle Clarkson's achievements in their father's biography. Even the *Times* newspaper called for Wilberforce's sons, one of whom was a bishop, to correct the facts. They agreed to do so to calm down the public outcry but they never actually got round to following through with their apology. For years researchers relied on their book on Wilberforce to understand the campaign against the slave trade. There were few testaments from the slaves themselves since they were forbidden to read or write and all Clarkson's extensive correspondence, relating to the abolition movement was burnt by his wife after his death. The full story was never told or available and so Clarkson was cut out of history.

Zerbanoo used the occasion of the unveiling of the plaque at Westminster Abbey to introduce the two families to each other.

There had been a distance between the ancestors of these two great men Clarkson and Wilberforce. I shall always treasure a letter from Clarkson's descendants thanking me

She set the record right in a book titled *Thomas Clarkson the Campaign Against the Slave Trade*, which she dedicated to Quaker community for being at the forefront of the abolit movement. Like Clarkson, who was a member of the Chur of England, and yet attended Quaker gatherings, she is a stro admirer of the Quakers and their work for human rights.

Zerbanoo presented little known facts about Clarkson i her book on his life and times, which was one of the best ke secrets in British history. He is now acclaimed as the father o modern campaigning. Clarkson's many pioneering technique made the anti-slave movement one of the most pressing politica issues of the eighteenth century. He corresponded regularly with over 400 abolitionists, drawing them into a nationwide network. He used a diagram of a slave ship as a picture that showed slaves chained like sardines in a tin. This picture was displayed in the homes of most abolitionists to make people aware of the inhuman atrocities inflicted on slaves. Women were also encouraged to wear anti-slavery hat-pins, brooches and necklaces. For once, fashion was being used for justice.

Clarkson encouraged artists like Turner, poets like Wordsworth and industrialists like Wedgewood to throw thei weight behind the abolition movement. He mastermindeᵈ the boycott of sugar and the use of honey as a substitute ᵇ nearly half a million people. Most importantly, he interviewᵈ thousands of sailors employed on the transatlantic slave tra Many were dumped in the Americas, as they were not nee on the return journey to England, with the cargo of sᵘ and tobacco. European slavers off-loaded the sailors or them as slaves, abandoning them to lives of degradatioᵑ desperation. The testaments of these sailors helped con for introducing the two families at the Westminster Abbey celebrations. It broke the ice and cemented a respect that should have always been there between these two giants of the abolition movement and their families.

Some years later, when Zerbanoo visited Westminster Abbey for a Commonwealth memorial service, she noticed a bunch of beautiful wild flowers left on the ground covering the plaque to Clarkson that simply said 'A Friend of Slaves'.

Zerbanoo considers Thomas Clarkson who started the world's first human rights organization, Anti-Slavery International, to be the noblest of Englishmen. She quotes poet Coleridge saying he was 'A moral steam engine'.

Upon being asked to co-chair the centenary celebrations of Dadabhai Naoroji, once again Zerbanoo was reminded of being inspired by an extraordinary life. She could identify with the man of unequivocal passion. Dadabhai Naoroji was the first South Asian member of the British parliament who faced similar setbacks and political sidelining as Zerbanoo did. It propelled her to pay a touching tribute to the triumph of human spirit in a book titled *Dadabhai Naoroji: Britain's First Asian MP*.

Known as the Grand Old Man of India, Dadabhai Naoroji was elected for the Liberals in the London seat of Finsbury Central in July 1892. He won the marginal seat by just five votes. Like Clarkson, he too was brought up by his widowed mother and belonged to a religious family. Both the fathers of Zerbanoo's heroes were priests. Naoroji's father, had been a Zoroastrian dastoor (priest) and Clarkson's father a Church of England vicar. They were morally righteous men. Both Naoroji and Clarkson were extraordinary men who inspired nations and fought inequality their entire lives.

Highlighting the lives of men with great strength of character and the spirit of benevolence served as the motivating factor not only for Zerbanoo but also for the British school children amongst whom her books were distributed. History is not just learning about the terrible mistakes made by leaders and their followers but also of inspirational individuals who changed the world by their trueness of purpose and goodness. She was keen to encourage young people to search for the hero within themselves.

The post-colonial guilt from the days of the Raj, when more than one half of the world was enslaved, has repercussions. Zerbanoo refers to bad karma being inescapable for individuals as well as for countries that have morally wronged others.

The Bible puts it perfectly: 'As you sow, so shall you reap.' When nations exploit and denigrate other people, there is no getting away from the karma they build up. Today, the West is hopelessly fighting obesity, alcoholism and drug addiction. It is so evident that there is no escape from karma. The British enslaved people and made them harvest sugar and tobacco under the most cruel conditions. They imposed opium on the Chinese and destroyed an ancient culture. Now it's a sweet revenge. Sugar is the new killer. It makes people obese and is the underlying problem to so many modern diseases. An injection of sugar into the bloodstream is similar to stimulating the pleasure centres of the brain that respond to heroin and cocaine. Cities are caught up in drug addiction.

Zerbanoo is convinced that when the slaves were working

on the plantations, they were bitterly cursing those who treated them inhumanly. She says, 'I believe that curses do have power.'

It took dogged persistence by Zerbanoo as the director of Anti-Slavery International to help raise the media awareness to current forms of slavery. She drew attention to millions of child slaves working in mines, factories, farms and brothels around the world. Lambasting sex tourism, she used the public platform to condemn the scale of exploitation that allows helpless children to be deprived of education, basic healthcare and love that goes into bringing up well-rounded individuals in society.

Using the media to generate awareness she was quoted:

> It is sad that so many politicians talk about the next generation but they rarely do anything about it. One half of children who are in indentured labour, and that number runs to millions, will die from accidents, disease and hunger before they reach twelve. Many are given drugs not as medicine to alleviate their pain but to stop them from running away. We need a 'slavery-free' labelling system just like we have cruelty-free products for animals and birds in the market today.

Not afraid of exposing those that misuse power, Zerbanoo has been relied upon by the media for crucial research material and stories ranging from the use of child soldiers, to women subjected to rape as a weapon of oppression in war. Joan Davies, the first woman to teach at the Sandhurst Military Academy, and someone who Zerbanoo worked with on the issue of female genital mutilation (and who later nominated

Zerbanoo for the *Good Housekeeping* Woman of the Century Award) explained:

> Zerbanoo is the opposite of an intellectual, elaborating abstract ideas with no action or results. She has an intellectual rigour. But, her ideas and action depend on moral decisions in a real world. She includes and involves others in great initiatives and always gives them credit. In today's world people like her are rare.

While most people would have been derailed by racial insults, Zerbanoo has often stood up against the cynical misuse of power. At the height of the 1987 general election, which she contested from East Harrow, a local newspaper published a letter saying that an immigrant like Zerbanoo should go back to her home country to contest elections there. Zerbanoo called the editor and made an appointment to see him. On meeting him, she objected to the public display of racism, especially from a ubiquitous 'Mr Smith' living on a non-existent road in Harrow. The editor argued that 'Mr Smith' was representing the national sentiment about foreign-born politicians. Zerbanoo told the editor off, accusing him of being utterly irresponsible for playing the race card.

On gauging the editor's mood and seeing that the discussion was going nowhere, she warned him that if he ever printed a letter instigating racism, she would make sure his paper was never sold. Nearly all the newsagents in Harrow were Indians. She informed the editor in no uncertain terms that if she asked the newsagents to stop selling the paper, for which the profit margin was very small, they would. It worked. The editor never published another racist article or letter.

On another occasion, Zerbanoo was speaking at a large campaign rally and a voice from the far end of the auditorium started hurling abuse at her. The man shouted, 'You bitch, you should be a member of the Labour party. It was Labour that gave India Independence.'

The audience was palpably shocked and dumbfounded at the rude interruption. Whilst anyone else would have been understandably tongue-tied by such a hostile attack in public, Zerbanoo fired back: 'It wasn't any political party in Britain that gave India Independence. Millions of Indians died for freedom.'

So saying, she calmly continued with the speech that won a huge applause.

In order to give her some respite from political rallying, her husband, Richard, asked Zerbanoo to accompany him to Uganda for a legal case he was undertaking. It was a period of great strife and turmoil, in the early eighties in Uganda. Not the best time to be there. When Zerbanoo made an excursion to Jinja, to see where many successful East African Indians had lived, she was escorted in a Mercedes by armed guards to protect her from roaming bandits. She still shudders at the memory of living at the Nile Palace in Kampala. It bothered her to sleep in Idi Amin's bed in his state rooms. Being very sensitive to places that have had a troubled past, she could feel that the bed of the crazed dictator, 'known as the butcher of Uganda,' was unclean. She slept on the floor instead.

On the way back to England, Richard decided to stop off in Kenya to have the much-needed break they deserved. It was a big mistake. There was some more drama as Zerbanoo was stopped at the Nairobi airport because her British passport showed her country of birth as India. It annoyed her to see her husband with the same British passport breeze through immigration, while she was detained, quizzed and not allowed to proceed. Initially, the official refused to say why she was barred from entry. Later, they discovered that the official held her back because he suspected she might be refused entry at Heathrow Airport because her British passport showed her place of birth as India. Only after a humiliating search for documents that proved she was an elected politician in Britain, was she eventually allowed entry into Nairobi for a night.

Zerbanoo used her experience to alert people in Britain. A month later at the Liberal Party conference at Eastbourne, she held up two passports and asked the audience if they could tell the difference. Then dramatically to the cameras she announced: 'This one belongs to my husband Richard and it works and this one belongs to me and it doesn't.'

It was used on the evening newsflash and led to an appraisal of how British passports of those not born in England were viewed differently in other countries, especially Africa.

Her connection with Africa goes way beyond the passport episode. An active member of the Anti-Apartheid Movement, she had the honour to speak, in the early eighties, at Trafalgar Square with Lord Kinnock, then leader of the Labour Party, to an audience of over 25,000 people. Later, she was chosen with Bishop Trevor Huddleston to hand in a massive peoples' petition to 10 Downing Street, which urged the then prime minister, Margaret Thatcher to stop the massacres in South Africa, apply full mandatory sanctions against the apartheid government there and call for the release of Nelson Mandela.

While Zerbanoo has courageously fought the equality battle

in full public glare, she has been fortunate to be married to a human rights lawyer who feels as strongly about extreme acts of discrimination. For the past twenty years, Richard has been fighting one of the most iniquitous modern crimes against humanity. He has been challenging the illegal expulsion, in 1968, by the British Government, of the Chagossians, the indigenous inhabitants of the island of Diego Garcia and other islands of the British Indian Ocean Territory. Today, Diego Garcia is a US military base.

Zerbanoo takes great pride in the pro bono work he does and his single-minded determination to see justice prevail for the Chagossian people.

Richard's legal campaign has not only been conducted in London, but also in Washington, Strasbourg and Mauritius and through this, Richard and Zerbanoo struck up a lifetime friendship with the international lawyer, Robin Mardemootoo. Zerbanoo says:

> Robin is one of those rare problem solvers. Although he practises in a world of high finance and law, he has established the human rights initiative SPEAK to challenge governments who abuse human rights anywhere in the world. Richard and Robin planned a marathon legal campaign for the Chagos islanders. Focused determination and selflessness will surely triumph. Recently Amal Clooney, wife of actor George Clooney, has joined the legal team with her expertise on International Human Rights.

Zerbanoo also talks, with great warmth, of the former deputy prime minister of Mauritius, Sir Gaetan Duval, a rare politician who was irrepressibly flamboyant and actually loved by his people. Sir Gaetan stayed with Zerbanoo and Richard at their home in Harrow-on-the-Hill in 1996 during his last visit to Europe before he died. Zerbanoo was his official cabbie and guide, and she takes pride in saying that she could have easily been a London taxi driver considering the number of people she has driven around London.

When it came to her own political career pathway, Zerbanoo discovered some bitter home truths. Whilst the Liberal party was radical when she first joined it, she slowly learnt that the empowerment of women and minorities was just another issue. Few other politicians had the same passion. They casually elbowed it out, just like they did to her sense of optimism. The disillusionment had set in for a while and it was beginning to show. In one of her national interviews, she revealed the source of her conflict and frustration. She was quoted as saying:

At the end of the day, it was the song and not the singer. They were all white, middle-class men who just wanted to win elections.

They insisted you sang their song however self-serving and foolish the words were. Everybody tells you that in order to change things you've got to be part of the establishment. Fair enough, but you spend so much time and energy becoming part of the establishment that you lose the reasons why you joined in the first place. You end up being what you sought to replace. There must be a way an individual can stand up for themselves and say that this is wrong, and I want to change it, now.

Using her political column to express her forthright views, Zerbanoo admits that being in British politics was important for her to understand how power is used and misused. After fifteen years of dedicated work, it was time to leave party politics.

She thinks Britain has little moral authority to lecture the world about democracy when its own second chamber, the House of Lords, is unelected.

> There have been peers sent to prison and when they come out of jail are able to return to the House of Lords and legislate for us. The recent expenses scandal in Britain highlighted the contempt a number of peers have for the rule of law and self-regulation. For them public service has become self-service. They are shameless and the system underpins their lack of morality. They have lost the respect of right-minded people. It is farcical and yet no one will reform the House of Lords. Those in power like it as it is, filled with former politicians, civil servants, their mates and those who use their wealth to support political parties to ensure their place in the Upper House. Some of them think it is a dining club that they need to belong to and for others it is a retirement home where they are paid for showing up. No wonder the young feel disfranchised and totally alienated from a political system that manipulates democracy. People who legislate for others should have the integrity to stand for elections and return regularly for endorsement of their work. A job for life is a thing of the past.

One of the theories behind Zerbanoo being ruthlessly undermined by her own party members and those in positions of power comes from Dr Megighian:

She was a risk to the established system, not because she is a radical, but just because she has always proven right in her views. It is a capital sin for a woman to articulate the feelings and fury of good people disenchanted with the political system. It amounts to witchcraft. Unfortunately, she could not be burnt alive, so she has been politically defused.

Author and contemporary commentator, Professor Alison Donnell believes it was her honesty that scared them. She says, 'Her principles were so pure, so simple they realized she couldn't be bought over. That perhaps didn't sit very well with those in power.'

The leader of the House of Lords, the Baroness Royall of Blaisdon, agrees that Zerbanoo posed a serious threat to her contemporaries. The astute politician surmises:

Zerbanoo is a great loss to the democratic system in Britain and should have been a Member of Parliament. Zerbanoo was a powerful woman at a time when men were not used to having strong women in politics. They would have been threatened by her strength. She was let down by the Liberal Democrats. I think it was wrong. Strength and the power went against her. Women were jealous and men were afraid.

After devoting more than fifteen years of her life to politics, Zerbanoo found another context for her true values that she could translate into reality. It was time to reinvent herself. To follow her unique purpose and allow her spirit to seek a different expression far bigger than anything she had ever imagined was achievable in the political arena.

TEN

LADY DHARAMSHALA

One of the more touching stories of the first Mughal emperor to rule India is veined with the purity of unconditional love. When Emperor Babar's son, Humayun fell seriously ill, the king was heartbroken. Royal physicians tried every cure possible but nothing seemed to work. Desperate to save his beloved son's life, Babar finally called on the most pious man in the kingdom for advice. The wise old man advised Babar to give up something that was most precious to him in exchange for his son's life. He hinted at the rose-tinted Kohinoor diamond in the emperor's possession and suggested that he sell it and donate the money to the poor. The Kohinoor is the world's most fought-over diamond, which now adorns the crown of Queen Victoria, safely encased in the Tower of London. It is said to be so valuable that it can feed the entire world for two-and-a-half days.

Emperor Babar spent sleepless nights but, finally, he realized that his own life was far more precious than the Kohinoor diamond. The mighty emperor was willing to sacrifice himself to save the life of his son, the rightful successor to his throne.

Having arrived at this brave decision, he circled his dying son's bed three times, beseeching Allah to take his own life instead of his son's. He prayed fervently: 'Let me die in his place, and let him live on earth. This is my most willing sacrifice.'

His prayers were answered. Within minutes, Humayun's pulse returned to normal. Sadly, the king fell seriously ill. Three months later, he breathed his last, leaving his kingdom to the son he so cherished.

This story was narrated to me by a well-wisher of Zerbanoo's who had worked on a major project with her. She told me how hard she had prayed for Zerbanoo on hearing about her dreadful car accident on the morning of 23 September 2009 as Zerbanoo was driving to work.

> The doctors thought we might lose her. I felt that Zerbanoo's life was far more precious than mine. She needs to be alive. She has made such a big difference to so many people's lives. I prayed to God to take my life instead, like Babar when he prayed for his son Humayun's life.

This heartfelt revelation indicated the extent to which Zerbanoo's friends go to express their love for her. A wide spectrum of people shared compelling stories and experiences of how Zerbanoo had impacted their lives. It is impossible to weave in every story but a couple of narratives give an insight into the emotional dynamics that shape lives.

Long after Zerbanoo's younger sister Genie sold the family hotel when their father passed away, the innate flair for hospitality stayed with Zerbanoo. Everyone who knocked at her door was given a bed, a hearty meal and a roof over their head. At times, they didn't even have to knock. With so many houseguests throughout the year, Richard couldn't walk down the corridor in his own home, without bumping into someone his wife had invited to stay. It once led Richard to take his big-hearted wife aside and request her, in all earnestness, to keep at least one bedroom available for him.

It explains how the label of Lady Dharamshala came to be. Fionnuala McHugh, a seasoned journalist now based in Hong Kong, chuckles as she recounts her wonderful experience:

> It was Zerbanoo who told me what the word, 'dharamshala', meant. According to her personal dictionary, it is a resting place, a sanctuary for anyone who comes your way, and that is exactly what her home, Herga House, became for so many people.
>
> In more traditional terms, a dharamshala is an Indian charitable rest house for travellers.

The list of houseguests, besides students and the homeless, also included the grand and the great who popped in for sleepovers. They were soon included in the family embrace and were occasionally put to work. Anyone who knows Zerbanoo is aware of her penchant of giving every man a job, big or small. Nobody was exempt; not even the late Sohrab Godrej, one of India's leading industrialists who once absentmindedly walked on to the living room carpet with muddy shoes. Operation Dirt was promptly put into action. Out came the vacuum cleaner with a specific request to Mr Godrej to clean up his mess.

For someone who had never used a 'hoover', the business magnate was tickled pink and even grateful for the impromptu lesson in good housekeeping. Although the last thing Zerbanoo expected was the unusual request that followed: 'I want to be under house arrest at your home.'

He enjoyed living in the guest bedroom that overlooked an exquisite English garden tended by Zerbanoo's neighbour, Tony Beresford, the chairman of Heinz. Sohrab Godrej enjoyed being treated like family without anyone fussing over him and often drove straight from the Heathrow Airport to Herga House. He preferred living at the Gifford home to a five star hotel. Richard often drove him straight to visit the Queen's cousin, the Bowes-Lyon family with whom he had a close bond.

Even though Sohrab Godrej was entertained by royalty, he was prudent enough to know that less is more. A simple man at heart, he always travelled light. All he carried was an Air India cabin bag whenever he visited Herga House. It contained just the bare necessities – a toothbrush, a razor, underwear and a pair of socks which he dutifully hand washed himself and laid out to dry. He gave Zerbanoo useful tips about travelling light saying how much does one need after all, and shared incredible life experiences with her.

Annabelle Cyprus Boal, known to Zerbanoo as Pana, an old Roedean school friend and one of her bridesmaids, stayed with her for almost a year. Pana and her husband John had bought a house adjoining the Giffords'. When they sold their house in Oxford, they needed a place to stay while their new home in Harrow-on-the-Hill, was being refurbished.

Zerbanoo kindly offered our family with two children space to stay on the top floor flat of Herga House. It meant a lot to us. We stayed there till our house was done up, which nearly took a year.

She is no fair weather friend. It was not just us. I remember Polly, who was a long-staying guest at her dad's hotel, also lived with Zerbanoo. When Polly was old and ill, Zerbanoo out of her own accord, brought Polly into her own home, nursed and looked after her till the very end. It wasn't pleasant when she died, but Zerbanoo cared for her.

Zerbanoo's sister Genie thinks Zerbanoo was like the passionate suffragette mother Mrs Banks from the film *Mary Poppins*.

[Mrs Banks] lived in this gorgeous Victorian villa with her two lively children and Mr Banks, a perfect gentleman, who had a clear daily rhythm to his life and a definite sense of order. Richard and Zerbanoo could easily play those parts in a modern-day version for Disney. When Richard came home every evening around the same time, Zerbanoo was always there to welcome him even though she had had a busy day dashing around empowering women. Everyone deferred to Richard. It didn't matter how many people were staying or who they were, Richard was boss. Of course, he was always so gracious and accommodating to Zerbanoo's endless stream of friends. I think the whole world must have stayed at their home, Herga House, at one time or another.

Projecting kindness into the universe is a virtue that both Zerbanoo's sons Mark and Alexander imbued at an early age. Mark met Cyprian Onderi, an ace javelin-thrower, whilst working at the charity Minorities of Europe, in Coventry. Seeing Cyprian struggling to make ends meet, Mark rang his mum asking if she could sponsor the Kenyan for a maths degree at the Coventry University. Although Zerbanoo was not keen since she was already inundated with too many responsibilities, she ended up welcoming Cyprian into the family fold.

Like so many foreign students from a disadvantaged background, Cyprian arrived in England to study and, within no time, the challenges of being in a new country hit him hard. Luckily for him, he was introduced to 'a hard-headed, soft and big-hearted lady', as Rustom describes his sister. According to Cyprian:

Zerbanoo always treated me like a son. She organized the funding of my tuition fees and found me accommodation. There is no amount of work I could have done to ever repay her generosity. I was also welcomed at her home and the ASHA Centre during the holidays and was treated with so much thoughtfulness by everyone. Even my own mother wasn't there but Zerbanoo made it a point to be with me on my graduation day. I can never forget that day. It was a long drive and raining heavily when we left for my graduation ceremony in Coventry. We had to make an early start at 5 a.m. and Zerbanoo was panicking that we may not make it on time. Luckily, we arrived just in time at Coventry cathedral. I finally received my degree, which was my passport to a new life, after four years of hard work. Zerbanoo just hugged me with such delight. We had done it.

There are several things that Cyprian learnt from Zerbanoo starting from making a perfect bed, punctuality and picking up the rhythm of biodynamic gardening. He discovered how 'tough love' has the potential to turn a life around. Cyprian is convinced that the training he received from Zerbanoo was a good warm-up for life in the British armed forces. There were the many times when Cyprian experienced the golden heart beneath the tough exterior and he echoes the sentiments of all those who shared their stories with me.

Zerbanoo is disciplined. She will tell you off to your face if you do something wrong. If it is raining outside and the garden needs digging she will put on her boots and lead by example.

I learnt from her that if something has to be done, you do it regardless of how tired you are or how miserable the weather is. Similarly, in the army we have to go out even if it is very cold or early. If a job has to be done however tough, you just do it. I shall never forget the time that the ASHA Centre was hosting women doctors and teachers from the refugee camps in Palestine. The women were being transformed and you could see their new-found confidence. There was a particular scene with an older Palestinian man who was misusing his position as their guardian to embarrass one of the women. Zerbanoo pulled him out of the dining room, and dealt with him before you could blink an eye. He called her the General after that.

Zerbanoo has been caring not only for me but for so many people. There is a group of extremely challenged kids who come to ASHA from St. Christopher's School every week. Some of them have severe problems. Zerbanoo noticed it and made a special effort to build a spacious washroom for them so that they would be more at ease.

Isabel Morgan, a childhood friend, shares another anecdote. Isabel, a bright student, was an unwitting victim of the social class barriers in Britain during the swinging sixties. When Isabel applied for admission to the hallowed Oxford University, she faced opposition from her headmistress who tore up her application form into little bits. She insulted Isabel for having the audacity to dream of Oxford when her mother couldn't even afford to buy her a decent school uniform. Determined to pursue further studies, Isabel sent another application to St. Hugh's College, Oxford and was called for an interview. Her headmistress had made her nervous and conscious of the fact that her family wasn't wealthy enough for the elitist Oxford College. Her mother had to pawn the family clock to buy her train ticket to Oxford so she could attend the entrance interview.

It was sheer coincidence that Zerbanoo breezed in to visit a friend who also babysat her brothers and sister to earn pocket money. Upon hearing that Isabel was about to leave for the much-awaited interview, Zerbanoo literally took the expensive coat off her back and gave it to Isabel who was worried about not having the right clothes to impress the interviewers at Oxford. She also slipped off her gold bracelet and gave it to Isabel to boost her confidence and wished her good luck saying, 'I would like to see who won't want you to join their college. Oxford would be crazy not to grab you.'

The thoughtful gesture instilled self-confidence in Isabel, and nearly fifty years later she recollects with a smile, 'I remember one of my friends saying, "you look so posh, so fabulous."'

It puts into context the words of the African American writer and poet Maya Angelou, 'People will forget what you said or what you did, but people will never forget how you made them feel.'

Indian-born Roshan Lala formerly worked with the cosmetic czarina of India, Simone Tata. When Roshan applied for immigration to Canada, she was summoned for an interview in London. She decided to take Zerbanoo up on her offer and stay at her place as she needed to get her paperwork done before she flew to Canada. She says, 'Realizing how nervous I was, Zerbanoo drove me to Quebec House and sweetly waited outside for three hours till I finished the process. Next day, we collected the requisite papers from the Federal office and went shopping.'

Just when they thought that all the tedious formalities had been done with, there was an unfortunate incident: Roshan's handbag with all its valuable contents was stolen while she was shopping at Selfridges, the Oxford Street department store. To her horror, she discovered that she had lost everything including her bank statement, documents, passport and visa. It was a nightmare as they rushed back to Quebec House and to the Indian Embassy to apply for a new passport and the concomitant paperwork redone.

Zerbanoo helped me with the documentation all over again although she wanted to kill the thief and me for being careless. It is because of Richard and Zerbanoo that I got my permanent citizenship. I used to stay with them and it was helpful for my Canadian visa application to speak French. In an attempt to improve my French, Richard, who speaks 'Un bon François' used to have conversations with me in French during breakfast to prepare me for questions I might have to answer at my immigration interview.

The High Commissioner of Seychelles, His Excellency Bob Delpech, calls Zerbanoo his guardian angel who reached out to him with compassion that helped him transcend pain.

She has been my angel who stood next to me and put my mind at peace. When my wife of forty-six years died, I was really low. The first thing Zerbanoo said was if you are depressed, jump in your car and drive down to me from Wales. You are always welcome to stay with us. Her home is very spiritual and it was so comforting in my moment of despair. Although my kids love me and my family is wonderful, I found solace in Zerbanoo's home. She helped me to face the world again. I would do anything for her. On my ninetieth birthday, she threw a big party for me. Now she is determined that my 100th birthday bash will be even bigger and more fun.

Bob met Zerbanoo in 1983 at the CHOGM (Commonwealth Heads of Government Meeting), which was being attended by the two most powerful women of the world at the time, Prime Minister Margaret Thatcher and hosting prime minister, Indira

Gandhi. Nevertheless, the woman who left a lasting impression on him during that conference was Zerbanoo. On spotting her at the CHOGM dinner for foreign ministers, Bob thought she looked familiar. As they chatted, they discovered that they both lived in Harrow and that he had seen her photographs almost every week in the local papers. They became instant friends. Years later, after Bob retired, he helped Richard in his fight to champion the cause of the displaced Chagossians.

Who would have thought that my friendship with Bob Delpech would help the Chagos people? It's as if God shrewdly planned our meeting in Delhi knowing the years later we would work together to fight a modern day injustice.

Bob was one of the few people who spoke a particular language, Patwa, spoken by the Chagossians. He was able to take evidence from the Islanders who had been exiled in Seychelles. It was because of his position in the diplomatic corps that he was able to address public meetings and help in the campaign. His contribution was invaluable.

Certain people come into our lives providentially. When Kirsten Rausing, one of the richest women in the world, heard Zerbanoo speak about the work being carried out at the ASHA Centre, she sent her a generous cheque without asking for any project reports or feasibility studies. Kirsten instinctively valued the groundbreaking work at ASHA with the young from all over the world. She trusted her money would be put to good use. That, to Zerbanoo, is true magnanimity.

Vishal Jadeja, Prince of Morvi, a former Bollywood producer and close neighbour of Zerbanoo's, has renounced a life of privilege to build a care home in Gloucestershire for people with learning disabilities. He gives his views on Zerbanoo's genius for philanthropic networking: 'When you serve a cause bigger than yourself, you gain a quiet power and ability to influence others. Zerbanoo's rare openness and willingness to engage with everyone for the benefit of the wider community makes her the perfect catalyst to carry out great change in this world.'

In the early years of ASHA, Zerbanoo attended a police award ceremony. Her brother Rustom was being presented with a medal for having saved a man's life at the Fulham football grounds. For many years, Rustom had been a Special Constable and had given his time freely to police London. Proud of her brother's act of courage, Zerbanoo was there to honour him. She was seated next to one of England's most famous footballers, Kevin Keegan, coach of Fulham and England.

As she started talking to him, she asked him whether he would be able to arrange for Fulham to play a friendly match to collect funds for ASHA, a newly established charity. Before she knew it, she was friends with Kevin Keegan and Chief Superintendent Anthony Wills of Hammersmith and Fulham. The two influential men were able to persuade the owner of the club, Mohamed Al Fayed, also the owner of Harrods and the father of Dodi who died with Diana Princess of Wales in that fateful car crash, to help Zerbanoo. A few months later, there was a friendly match between Israel's National Football team and Fulham to help fund the work of ASHA with young people.

Driven by the constant desire to reach out to people, upon hearing from her friend, impresario Shireen Isal, about Father Fonseca and his home for street children in Mumbai, Zerbanoo couldn't wait to meet Father Fonseca on her trip to India. She asked Father Fons (as she calls him) and his children what they would like her to bring for them. The street children unanimously voted for toys with which they could play together as a group. They decided on a box set of Lego and a television set. Zerbanoo immediately had a television installed in the children's home.

Prior to her next trip to India, Zerbanoo called the marketing manager of Lego in London and told him of the street children and their special wish. The very next day, there were twenty-five gigantic Lego boxes delivered. Another call was made to her generous friend, Happy Minwalla, who arranged for her to see the head of Qatar Airlines. The airline allowed her excess baggage without any extra charge on her flight to India.

However, upon her arrival at Mumbai's Chhatrapati Shivaji International Airport, Zerbanoo was stopped at the customs. The custom officer accused her of being a toy smuggler. Zerbanoo was not amused. She summoned the head of customs and read him the riot act for not doing enough for disadvantaged street children and hindering those who wanted to help. It goes without saying, the chief of customs was only too relieved to see her walk through the green channel.

ELEVEN

A NEAR-DEATH EXPERIENCE

A near-death experience is a mysterious phenomenon. The prism of human existence and death has always been a fascinating subject, juxtaposed with two scenarios playing out simultaneously in the theatre of life. In one, the roller-coaster ride of life suddenly nose-dives to an all-time low as the light drains out of a person on the threshold of making the final journey. In the other, supernatural experience elevates the spirit to a higher consciousness, riding high on waves of pure joy and ecstasy. It is utter bliss, the ultimate moment of truth as one's life's purpose gets unravelled in flashes of brilliance.

A near-death experience often gives a glimpse of the afterlife. Sceptics argue that any near-death experience could make the mind play silly tricks. It could be the effect of the brain's neurotransmitters shutting down, creating a kaleidoscopic illusion of sorts. Yet, no one has been able to come up with a plausible explanation for the conversation with God (or a divine presence) reported by most people who have gone through the surreal experience. It seems unlikely that so many people across cultures and countries have invented similar life-changing stories of being enlightened and touched by divinity.

A near-death experience for Zerbanoo was an intensely moving and transformative trip to heaven and back.

Richard and Zerbanoo had driven to Durham University, where Mark, their elder son, had just begun his degree in theology. Mark, a skilled drummer, had asked his parents to bring his drumkit to him so that he could practise while at university.

Just a week before that long drive, Zerbanoo had undergone the removal of a polyp in her bowel. Despite the discomfort, she was determined to make sure Mark had his drums. She also wanted to see Mark taking part in a fencing training session. It was while watching Mark fence that Zerbanoo started to bleed profusely. Richard realized something was terribly wrong. They quickly said goodbye to Mark and started the mad dash back to London.

Richard still recalls the horror of seeing Zerbanoo haemorrhage. The journey which usually took hours from the north-east of England was halved as he drove at over a hundred miles an hour down the old Roman A1 Road to the Royal Free Hospital in Hampstead, London. Zerbanoo had for many years been a registered patient there due to her rare bleeding disorder. For once in his life, Richard had hoped the police would have stopped him and given him an escort, but the road was clear. It weighed heavily on him that time was running out with the car soaked in blood and Zerbanoo nearly unconscious.

When Richard finally carried Zerbanoo into casualty, the doctor on duty announced it was a Saturday night and there was not a single bed available. The place was full of drunks and revellers, all the worse for wear. The doctor tried hard to persuade Richard to take her home to rest.

By that time, Zerbanoo's mother, Kitty, and sister Genie, had also arrived and immediately began pleading with the doctor to keep her in hospital, as they knew she would not survive the excessive bleeding if she were driven home. Zerbanoo's blood count had dipped to below three. She was ashen and ice cold. As Genie recalls: 'It was touch and go. Another doctor arrived and took us into a separate room and told us that Zerbanoo may not make it. She was clinically dead in his opinion. They were preparing us for the inevitable.'

The consent forms for surgery were drawn out as the medical staff went through the procedure of asking Richard if he would donate his wife's vital organs. Although he knew that Zerbanoo had given permission for her organs to be transplanted to help someone else live, Richard hesitated. But before he could respond, Kitty bluntly refused to allow the doctor to operate on her daughter. Richard was also aware that if they performed surgery, Zerbanoo would not survive the blood loss, and reiterated Kitty's stand.

For Kitty, it was a nightmare come back to haunt her as it seemed to be a flashback of all the horrors of her mother, Jerbanoo's death. She had bled to death following a simple tooth extraction at the age of forty-three. It seemed like it was no coincidence that Zerbanoo, named after her, was also forty-three. Sick with worry, Kitty was understandably livid when she overheard one of the doctors mentioning they had given up hope on reviving Zerbanoo because a match for her rare blood type was just not available.

There was a clever Indian doctor who was trying to help. I overheard him saying, 'Zerbanoo is "moribund".' I didn't know what it meant so I asked a nurse and she said, 'almost dead'. I couldn't believe that they had just given up on my child without getting the blood she so badly needed. I was enraged. I firmly told them not to wait for the exact blood group because there was no perfect match. They should immediately just give her a transfusion with the nearest match available and at least get her blood count up.

Genie causally let drop that Richard, a prominent lawyer, specialized in hospital negligence cases and that he wouldn't take anything happening to his wife lightly. Kitty adds: 'Had I not created a ruckus, the blood would have never arrived by helicopter from a hospital in Birmingham.'

The family frantically called Zerbanoo's brother Rustom, who was in Syria at the time shooting the *Water Wars* programme for the BBC. He dropped everything and returned to London immediately.

I remember so clearly I was in Damascus and got the call that Zerbanoo was dying. I took the first plane back to England. Not easy in those days. I spent nights sleeping on the hospital floor near her bed since the hospital didn't have any facilities for relatives to stay. I didn't want my sister to be left alone all through the night with no one to care for her. She had needles and drips all over her and was in excruciating pain. She was very brave.

Richard couldn't bear to see his wife lying unconscious. His way of dealing with the trauma was to excuse himself and go home to look after their younger son, Alexander.

For all intents and purposes, Zerbanoo was clinically dead; however, in her subconscious she had been catapulted to an alternative reality. Her entire being was awash with a sense of peace and she felt incredibly free and light. The excruciating pain was replaced by the warm glow of a golden light that suffused her entire being with luminescence. It felt like being embraced by a sunbeam with a million specks of shimmering stardust.

Now I know what it is to die. I was cradled in a world where time and space seemed to vanish. It was an amazing feeling. I distinctly remember seeing an exquisite golden chariot being driven by Lord Krishna, the Hindu god known as the embodiment of love and joy. I could feel his divine presence. I had often visited the Hare Krishna Temple in Letchmore Heath near London to meditate and enjoy the beauty and tranquillity of the centre. Now, being in this other world, I could feel Lord Krishna's overwhelming, yet gentle presence. He had enfolded me in an embrace and was holding me in front of him as he drove the chariot, whispering that I could not give up. I had still not gone into battle. I remember wanting to just collapse into his strength and close my eyes forever, it was bliss being in his divine aura. Then I felt him guide me back to life, with the words: 'There is no time to rest.'

The doctors and nurses who seemed to have given up on Zerbanoo, watched with amazement as she miraculously regained consciousness and her blood count started ascending. There was a very good reason she had returned to the land of the living. In time, she would come to find the clarity and strength to embrace her special destiny. It was a surreal wakeup call by destiny for Zerbanoo to inspire the next generation of world leaders to find their own greatness.

Adding an uncanny twist to the story was a doctor friend of Zerbanoo's who had a premonition at precisely the same time. He sensed that she was unwell and called to inquire after her health. He knew it was more than a coincidence that he had seen an inexplicable apparition of Zerbanoo being cradled in the arms of Lord Krishna in a golden chariot, preparing to go into battle. There was no logical explanation for his vision.

Zerbanoo was not afraid of dying:

I have a great belief that there is a predetermined time span and no one can interfere with that. Obviously, my time on earth was not finished. I do not believe that anyone really dies forever. People just go and have a long rest before they come back to continue their struggle to make this world a better place. I am sure we have all made a soul contract with God to do something magnificent while living. Most of us just forget that and act foolishly. I am in no doubt that we will all have to face the Day of Judgment. I think we will be given the opportunity to look at a big screen and watch all the people who have impacted our lives and how we interacted with them. We will experience all the joy, as well as the heartaches we have given others. There is no escape for anyone from the Laws and the Lords of Karma who record everything.

Whatever we say or do and even our thoughts go into the universe. There is also such a thing as instant karma. You don't have to wait for another lifetime or a rebirth to reap the consequences or the rewards. It is there for all to see. You just have to be observant and see how life for yourself and others unfolds.

A classic example of redeeming instant 'karmic points' was when Zerbanoo was first refused entry into the hospital. Although no beds were initially available, a casualty nurse appeared from nowhere within a short span of time, and upon seeing Zerbanoo, asked if she was the same public personality featured in the media. The minute she knew who Zerbanoo was, she jumped into action. Apparently, many years ago, Zerbanoo had helped her get a student loan.

The senior nurse told Kitty that Zerbanoo had come to her rescue during a crisis when she was a young student, struggling financially to pursue her career in nursing. Zerbanoo had used her political office to source a grant for her medical studies. The nurse had always wanted to personally thank her for what she had done to transform her life. Kitty believes that Zerbanoo is a living testimony to the fact that the universe pays you back in this lifetime. Whatever good you do, always comes back to you in the most unexpected ways.

At the first sign of recovery, Zerbanoo, who had missed out on her schedule of speaking engagements due to her sudden hospitalization, reverted to her usual self, pulling out all stops. A press statement in the *Liberal Democrat News* dated the 12 November 1993 reads:

Zerbanoo Gifford was admitted to the haemophilia centre at the Royal Free Hospital as an emergency last weekend following complications after an operation to remove a malignant polyp from her colon. She remains in serious condition but is expected to recover to continue the fight against the Tories by Christmas. All her appointments for the next few weeks have been cancelled, including speaking at the long list of Liberal Democrat meetings around the UK. 'I'm sorry to have to postpone everyone,' she said from her hospital bed. 'On Harrow council, the Tories said I was a bleeding heart Liberal. I'm glad to confirm this is still the case even though I sometimes wish I didn't bleed quite so much.'

With her signature humour, Zerbanoo states that if there is one thing she has in common with Prince Charles, it is that she cannot take anyone else's blood.

We rare individuals have to store our own blood in a blood bank in case we need a transfusion. I think that means we have blue blood or maybe we are just 'bloody' difficult to deal with. In any case, I have to live with this disability. It is a very rare condition known as Glanzmann thrombasthenia.

Zerbanoo's condition had come to light when she was only seven years old. No one took much notice when she hurt herself whilst having a pillow fight with her cousins. Her cousin Rohinten accidentally hit her on the mouth and her parents were aghast when the bleeding from the small wound would not stop despite trying everything. Panicking at the sight of Zerbanoo going pale, they rushed her to Great Ormond Street Children's Hospital in London. Many tests later, she was diagnosed with Glanzmann thrombasthenia, an extremely rare autosomal recessive disease in which the platelets do not produce clots in the normal way, causing haemorrhaging in response to a cut or perforation. Her parents knew they had to be extremely careful with their daughter to make sure she didn't fall or hurt herself in any way.

Zerbanoo's blood condition became the subject of a thesis by the renowned Dr Katharine Dormandy, who was working at the Great Ormond Street Children's Hospital at that time. A lifelong relationship developed between the doctor and her patient. Years later, the Haemophilia Centre and Thrombosis Unit at the Royal Free Hospital was named 'The Katharine Dormandy Haemophilia and Thrombosis Centre', one of the largest haemophilia treatment centres in Europe dealing with management of bleeding disorders. Zerbanoo helped with fundraising for the haemophilia centre through Dr Dormandy's lifetime.

Zerbanoo has also allowed herself to be used for research programmes in order to help other people with blood disorders have a better quality of life. On every occasion, she has used her experience to champion the cause of those with the disability – especially those with haemophilia who accidently received contaminated blood and went on to become HIV positive. A great deal of courage is needed to deal with a disability. In Zerbanoo's case, she has used a genetic disorder to encourage anyone who has a disappointment or disability to concentrate on his or her strengths and abilities and make the most of their life.

His wife's blood disorder had Richard worried even before they married. Prior to tying the knot, he fixed an appointment with her specialist, Dr Dormandy, to check if it would be safe for Zerbanoo to conceive. The prognosis was that they had no case history of any woman with a similar condition who had given birth. The specialist was more than keen to find out how her life would unfold medically, especially during menstruation and menopause, if Zerbanoo lived long enough.

The birth of their first-born was a worrying time for Richard and their family friend, Sir George Pinker, the Queen's gynaecologist and senior consultant at St. Mary's Hospital in Paddington. The hospital was made famous by Alexander Fleming, who discovered Penicillin on the very premises, furthermore, it is considered one of the top teaching hospitals in the world. It is also where many of Britain's modern royal family have been born, including Princess Diana's son William and William's children, Prince George and Princess Charlotte.

In the early hours of 28 August 1975, Zerbanoo was driven by Richard to St. Mary's Hospital from their first home, a little cottage in Harrow. Zerbanoo's water bag had broken. The anaesthetist was ready to give her an epidural, but suddenly refused to do so upon being told of Zerbanoo's extremely rare bleeding disorder of Glanzmann thrombasthenia.

The anaesthetist was worried that an injection into her spine might trigger her bleeding and end up causing paralysis. Zerbanoo was in such pain that she passed out and they had to use forceps to deliver Mark. She started to haemorrhage and lost four-and-a-half litres of blood. It happened so quickly Richard thought he might have to be both mother and father to his son, as his wife was slowly sinking. All Zerbanoo remembers of the fated morning when Mark arrived was that he was placed in her arms before she was rushed to the Intensive Care Unit.

Mark was so beautiful. In his eyes I saw that look of a very old soul. He didn't look particularly happy to be born again. The expression on his face said, 'I have seen this all before. Do I really have to go through it again?' We named our baby Mark because Richard used to call me his Zorro, and so he was to be my Mark of Zorro.

Fortunately, Zerbanoo had a relatively normal and easy delivery when Alexander, her second son, was born.

I was delivered by the wonderful National Health Service, but once again, Sir George took care of me throughout my pregnancy. I was taken into St. Mary's Hospital early so that my delivery would be monitored to avoid an emergency and unexpected drama. They gave me platelets and then broke my water to speed up the birth. I shall never forget Sir George telling me that I had better get on with it, as he was going skiing in San Moritz that evening and wanted to be present to hand me my new baby. The day went quite quickly as there were nine doctors coming in and out of my room waiting to see the outcome. I was completely distracted talking to them and couldn't remember much pain. All I can recollect is being held in Richard's arms trying to take deep breaths and thinking how much I was missing Mark. And then, there was Alexander in my arms. I looked into his eyes and thought: 'This is one of the happiest days of my life.'

TWELVE

THE STORY OF HOPE

Refusing to allow the regrets in her political journey to create mental roadblocks, Zerbanoo walked away from the petty party politics. The intervening years enabled her to make a paradigm shift. She believes, 'If you need to change paths, you can give yourself permission to just backtrack and try a new, more fulfilling one.'

An intuitive inkling that something needed to be done for the next generation of global leaders had already entered her thinking. Zerbanoo was inspired by something outside herself, although there was no definite plan in place yet.

In the past, whilst dealing with race-related and faith issues, she had often felt the need for an intercultural, multi-faith centre where people of all communities and faiths could freely celebrate their differences and rejoice at their similarities.

It was apparent that the Hindus had their centre and the Muslims, Christians, Sikh, Jews and Parsis had their individual places of worship but there was no common place that could bind them together; a place where people of any faith, or none, could meet. With all her heart and soul, she hoped for the impossible: 'If only there was a beautiful, sacred place where people in all their diversity could come together and share their stories; it would help to put an end to conflict and disharmony.'

The centre would highlight the contribution that all communities made to British life with a museum, faith gardens, theatre and a resource centre for schools. It would be an ode to multicultural London with an emphasis on education.

The golden opportunity to give wings to her desire came in the form of the Millennium Commission set up in Britain to celebrate the turn of the millennium. It was launched amidst great fanfare with funding of over two billion pounds raised through the UK National Lottery. The money was to be injected into buildings, environmental projects, celebrations and community schemes.

It was only at the eleventh hour that the Millennium Commission Committee realized that a pittance of the funding money had been allocated to ethnic minorities. They had a legal obligation to ensure that the money from the lottery was allocated to all the communities that made up Britain. In a rare nod to communal diversity, they announced the grant of ten million pounds to an ethnic minority-led project. It was up for grabs. The prerequisite condition for bidding was that the organization concerned had to raise an equal amount to match the funding granted to them.

It triggered a fierce race as different groups vied for the pot of gold. ASHA's objective was to establish a multifaith, multicultural centre available to all, but reflecting the contribution of the ethnic communities in Britain. The news that the ASHA Foundation started by Zerbanoo had been the selected charity spiralled into the top headlines of the day.

ASHA Foundation was welcomed by the Millennium Commission as a means of reflecting the evolving, multicultural face of Britain. It was felt that the proposed ASHA Centre would inject peace into the community and prosperity into the economy at a time when Britain was experiencing racial and religious disharmony.

The media was sympathetic towards the shortlisting of ASHA as the preferred charity for funding. One of the articles titled 'Ten Million Helps Tell Story of British Immigrants' in the *Times*, dated 08 November 1999, gave the details:

> The biggest National Lottery grant to an ethnic minority's project has been won by an Asian woman who will receive ten million pounds to create a museum celebrating immigration and Britain's many faiths. She has managed to persuade Muslims, Jews, Hindus and Christians to bury their differences in support of the 'ASHA Centre' which will teach about their history and beliefs. The award by the Millennium Commission emerges days after Tony Blair signed a pledge to defend multicultural values at a party celebrating Diwali, the Indian festival of lights.

The original ASHA Centre, which was going to be in London, would have housed a museum of migration, showing the richness of multicultural Britain. The blueprints envisioned faith gardens illustrating how in all religions, gardens are symbolic of man's relationship with the divine through nature. The well-designed layouts had earmarked a health zone as well as defined areas for a theatre, cinema and an international food court.

Zerbanoo's vision of peace and conflict-resolution had likeminded people stepping forward to give the required support. Plans were drawn up and a small army of committed enthusiasts worked frantically to tap prospective donors to raise equivalent funds to match the grant. Then, in an uncanny twist of events, everything came to a standstill. The bubble burst. Nine months down the line, Harrow Council, where the hoped-for centre would be built, took heed of the vehement protests of the local residents' association in the area. These residents were worried about possible traffic congestion problems that would be caused by Asian women driving large cars to Indian weddings at the new multicultural centre. In response, the council unceremoniously withdrew its support. This was done after half a million pounds had been sanctioned and spent on elaborate architectural building plans and a detailed feasibility study overseen by two international accountancy firms. The rug was pulled from under their feet as the Millennium Commission announced that the grant that had starred on their website was no longer 'attractive'.

The trustees at ASHA, who by then had secured redundant land belonging to the Ministry of Defence in North West London for the project and had paid a substantial deposit to buy the land, had no option but to sue the government agency PACE (the property advisors to the government office for commerce) for the volte-face on the legal sale of their land to ASHA. They also had to sue the Millennium Commission for reneging on their ten-million-pound grant to build the proposed ASHA Centre to the grand scale required for such a landmark project.

What was poised to be the much-awaited narrative of racial

and communal unity took an ugly turn. It was a harrowing time for Zerbanoo and everyone else involved in the project. Richard, who had always backed Zerbanoo's vision, valiantly stepped in and took over the tension overload. He had no option but to sue the government agency for going back on their word. It was no small matter to go to court against the full force of the entire British establishment.

Their son Mark, a qualified lawyer, pooled his time and knowledge to help his father. He says of the tough times the family faced:

> My father is a hero. I remember those huge bundles of documents that filled up our entire sitting room as we prepared for the court hearings. I wondered how Dad had the time or the energy to meticulously go through it all. I have seen him work every evening, after a gruelling day at the office and every weekend to prove we were in the right despite all kinds of allegations.

The family risked losing everything they had built, personally and professionally. Life became an exhausting stream of trials and tribulations, appeals and affidavits.

Although Zerbanoo has nerves of steel, she too was wracked by dark moments of anxiety. To overcome her unease, she decided to undertake a religious pilgrimage to India with the hope of seeking divine intervention. Her Godmother, Mappie, and her aunt, Hoshbanoo, her father's youngest sister, accompanied her to the Zoroastrian holy sites in India. They set off to pay homage at the eight Fire Temples known as Atash Behrams, where the original sacred fire still burns from thousands of years ago. There is a belief amongst those following the Zoroastrian faith that if one is able to visit all eight of these sacred places within a set time span, one's prayers are answered. It was not an easy task to accomplish as the Fire Temples are situated in two different Indian states, Gujarat and Maharashtra.

Determined to complete the pilgrimage in the time allotted, Zerbanoo set off on the sacred journey in a car. Both her godmother and aunt were religious, and would recite prayers throughout the journey. Like characters from Chaucer's Canterbury Tales, they also told Zerbanoo stories to keep her spirits up.

At her first stop, the Wadia Fire Temple in Mumbai, Zerbanoo felt an instant surge of divine energy. She went into a meditative trance as the dancing flames of the sacred fire cast a golden glow. She had a vision of two beautiful guardian angels on either side, holding her gently. Her whole being changed in a matter of seconds and she knew then that however many setbacks there would be, the ASHA Centre would come into being. Both her aunts commented on the change in her demeanour and difference in her aura.

As Zerbanoo stepped out of the Fire Temple, she collapsed into her eldest son's arms. Mark was waiting outside because he did not wish to offend the sensibilities of the orthodox Zoroastrians by entering the sacred Fire Temple. Mark held his mother tight and assured her that her wish had been granted and that the ASHA Centre would materialize. He says, 'My mother has an incredible drive and tremendous purity, and in her good moments she is used by a higher force to work through her. It enables her to achieve things that many people think is almost impossible.'

Zerbanoo continued her journey to the other seven Atash Behram/Fire Temples throughout Gujarat, and returned to Mumbai the next evening before sunset. She had accomplished her pilgrimage.

Upon her return to England, one of the first people she met was Edward Trevor, the respected civil servant in charge of disposing a number of properties. He recounts,

> I met Zerbanoo who came to see me to ask if she could have an acre of land for nothing in order to build a multicultural centre to promote peace and understanding amongst people of all nations, creeds and cultures. As the rules for government are that all land disposals have to be at the best price, I obviously said that it was not possible. Zerbanoo is not one to take 'No' for an answer when she has set her mind upon something; she will get it one way or another. She asked to see whoever was in charge and could sanction her request.
>
> A meeting was arranged for Zerbanoo. I was then instructed to obtain a valuation of the land in question. But there were difficulties as the land was in a Green Belt and close to extremely expensive houses where there would be considerable agitation against development. But there was an area of land nearby, in Honeypot Lane Harrow, with commercial zoning. I suggested that this was more likely to obtain planning permission for a Centre. Immediately Zerbanoo saw the sense in this and agreed, but still on the basis of nil or minimum payment.

To ensure that all went according to plan, the best professionals in London were employed. She was determined that the project for the Centre should proceed. Eventually, all plans and consents were in place and everyone was ready to go ahead. However, for purely political reasons, the government decided not to proceed; there was a general election in the not-too-distant future. Everyone believed that this was the end of the vision for the ASHA Centre. Notwithstanding this, Zerbanoo continued looking and never gave up hope. Eventually, she found a property in Gloucestershire, which was most suitable. It has now developed into the ASHA Centre, a place where peoples from all parts of the world regardless of religion, creed or colour meet.

Richard, who also played a crucial role in the creation of the ASHA Centre, explains that Zerbanoo's vision of a multicultural centre was extremely attractive and drew early support from every faith and ethnic minority community.

It was said that only Zerbanoo could bring them all together in a common cause. She approached the Millennium Commission when landmark projects were being sought. With a team of dedicated volunteers, the concept was rapidly endorsed by the cabinet office, the Millennium Commission and various local authorities who offered land for a site to house the project, which involved cutting-edge architecture.

After many sites had been analysed, and endless politicians consulted and cajoled, an optimum place was found in Harrow, coincidentally a local authority, where Zerbanoo had herself been a councillor and lived. The Millennium Commission earmarked ten million pounds for the project, subject to two main conditions: a feasibility study and matched funding, of which the value of land was to count at market value. Both the government and the local authority, to which a planning application was made, supported ASHA.

A year went by, during which an enormous feasibility study came in, demonstrating the viability of the centre. An application for planning permission was passed, even after opposition from a few local residents who feared an Asian takeover of a largely Jewish area – so much for the concept of multiculturalism in modern Britain.

The project was now set to go, but counter forces had been set up. The local Labour MP, who had been generous in supporting ASHA, now feared a voting backlash in an area where the voters were not his natural allies. He surreptitiously approached government departments and the Millennium Commission to seek the sinking of the ASHA project. The Millennium Commission, already suffering massive public discontent over the grandiose dome project, became risk averse. Without a word of explanation, or a single comment on the massive feasibility study, the Millennium Commission managed to veto the promised ten-million-pound grant. The government followed suit, plunging ASHA into three years of litigation with both defaulting former allies. And in this time also the precious and hard-won planning consent expired and its renewal was turned down.

But subsequent events have a strange irony. ASHA's efforts in the courts had failed to uphold the ten-million-pound grant, because the three judges felt that those handing out lottery money did not have to give any reasons for rejecting a project, even though they had previously supported an application and required the charity to spend half a million pounds on a feasibility study. Zerbanoo took the decision quite well, as she felt all the effort put into the case hadn't been totally wasted. She was very pleased when the Millennium Commission miraculously found another thirty million pounds after the case, which was earmarked only for ethnic minority projects. Up until then, they had received little or nothing from this huge lottery pot.

Zerbanoo admits to being devasted.

Of course I was devastated. We had lost the court case against the Millennium Commission and the funding after so much work especially since we had to pay off half a million pounds for a feasibility study, which we were obliged to undertake by them. I couldn't get over the outrageous amount of money wasted. We could have built a whole village for abandoned children in India for that sort of money. Then the Millennium Commission announced that we should reapply for this new pot of money, which they had miraculously found. I knew, having worked with people in power, that if you challenge them they make sure you are crushed. All the organizations who applied for this new lottery money received a grant. It pleased me that our efforts had not been in vain and other charities had benefitted from our courageous legal challenge of the Millenium Commisssion. The ASHA Foundation's application was the only one turned down. People in power are so predictable.

Richard continues:

Bereft of planning permission, the land we had bought with a bank loan had to be sold and produced strange consequences.

The proposed land that might have boasted gardens of tranquillity and great beauty now holds a ghastly development of box-like mini apartments, so numerous that the fears generated about Asian women coming in cars are comically underestimated. By contrast, a different ASHA Centre now graces the Forest of Dean, beloved of local residents, the local authority and the thousands of young people who come from all over the world to take in the ASHA experience.

It was quite by accident that Zerbanoo discovered the perfect spot for the ASHA Centre, from a chance meeting at a Murder Mystery weekend in Tunbridge Wells. She got chatting with a lively couple who were interested in issues around inter-faith matters. They never met again but kept in touch. Some years later, they suggested that Zerbanoo visit a property in the middle of the Royal Forest of Dean located in the county of Gloucestershire, England. It is called the Royal Forest since a large area had been reserved for royal hunting before 1066, and it remained the second largest Crown forest in England.

After five arduous years of searching for a perfect location, the charming, if run down, Georgian house seemed a perfect fit. The estate was being run as a bed-and-breakfast by the previous owners. A stream ran through it from the ancient St. Anthony's spring, once used by the monks of the neighbouring Flaxley Abbey. It had an ethereal feel about it. Zerbanoo telephoned her dear friend Berjis Daver, the former chairman of Ladbrokes, who selflessly helped her through the years of trying to build the ASHA Centre. He agreed to visit the site with her and immediately recommended she buy it.

Zerbanoo promptly rang her younger son, Alexander, a theatre director and scriptwriter, to check out the place, as he was at the time living not too far away, in Stroud. Alexander in turn asked a friend Adrian Locher, then director of Taurus Voice Theatre Company, to accompany him.

Adrian, going into a flashback of the days when he was a travelling actor/director, recalls: 'We jumped into the car and drove over.'

The moment couldn't have been more perfect for him. Adrian had been on the move for around fifteen years and was looking for a place to put down roots. It was as if the first piece of the jigsaw puzzle was finding its place in the larger scheme of things. No one had a clue what was in store. He smiles as he recounts with utmost clarity:

I remember it was March 2006. When we arrived at the house, Zerbanoo phoned Alex and asked if he would help her run it. Alex in turn asked me and I said 'Yes' without thinking; it came from within. It felt like a chance to fulfil my destiny. I do believe we are custodians of a very special site, the stream flowing through the estate from St. Anthony's sacred well and the protective embrace of the surrounding unspoilt forest. It is a place none of us would ever have thought of having a Centre. The minute I stepped into the place I felt – this is it.

From that moment onwards things started happening.

We stayed there, whilst the former owners were moving out. The transformation of the house and grounds began. We organized volunteering weekends to help clear the stream, pull the weeds and brambles, and remove the debris, even as everyone continued with their day time jobs.

Alexander and I, being from a theatre background, proposed to host the first programme at the Centre called 'Peace through the Performing Arts', producing plays each year with a mixed group of Jewish and Arab teenagers from Israel. Without hesitation, Zerbanoo said, in her usual generous way, 'Yes.' It was part of her dream to ensure young people were encouraged to be released from historical prejudice. She believed they had it in them to create possibilities and a peaceful future never imagined by their ancestors.

Right from the beginning, there was a hidden hand at work, guiding us and the plot. There was a strong sense of divine intervention, otherwise known as Grace. At every turn, the right person for the job appeared, like actors on cue. But we players certainly had to put in the hard work to learn our lines and moves. Zerbanoo, as lead actress, was too busy to learn her lines. She just improvised. She seems to enjoy altering her destined moves, with the permission, of course, of the original Scriptwriter. No doubt, he too applauds her spontaneity and ability to draw everyone into His magnificent play.

In 2007, we undertook the first Israeli project. Zerbanoo was supportive of the daring endeavour that took more than international diplomacy to realize it. We knew the Jewish drama teacher from the Harduf Kibbutz in northern Israel and he had been making links with a school in the neighbouring Arab town of Shef'ram. There was a lot of convincing to do since the parents of Arab girls were not very

keen to send the girls abroad. The Arab boys had to promise
to protect them. For our first production, we chose *Arabian
Nights*. It tells of a cruel king, who after listening to 1001
stories, falls in love with the beautiful young storyteller and
spares her life. For the young Jews and Arabs, who saw each
other as enemies, it had a potent message of the transforming
power of listening to each other's stories.

The script for *Arabian Nights* was riddled with plenty of real
life subplots that made the journey an unforgettable one. The
Jewish boys and girls were much more liberal in comparison to
the Arabs. Alexander narrated an episode that illustrated how
protective and possessive the Arab boys were of the Arab girls:

> One of the Arab boys fell in love with a Jewish girl; it was
> tough for all of us. There was an incident when some of the
> Arab boys took out their knives to threaten the Jewish boys.
> Fortunately, we had an ex-army commander with us who
> separated the two groups. We had to abandon rehearsals that
> day and work on conflict resolution, but it was an important
> part of the process.

These productions were not only successful artistic
achievements, but made a poignant social statement. When
Arabian Nights was performed in Israel, community leaders and
the Israeli press regarded it as the most meaningful contribution
to peace in the region for decades. For the first time, young
Arabs and Jews performed together on stage, watched by
families, who would otherwise not come within miles of each
other.

In an article that appeared in the *Times*, Avital Zohat, a seventeen-year-old Jewish girl, is quoted as saying: 'I was really happy when the Muslims joined in with our Sabbath prayers over Friday dinner at the ASHA Centre.'

Dr Frances Alexander, the founder of 'Women Welcome Women World Wide', former Mayor of High Wycombe and an old political comrade of Zerbanoo's, had the privilege of following the progress of the Israelis and Palestinians rehearsing *Arabian Nights*. She was highly impressed by the performance. Frances says it was an evening she won't forget for a long, long time.

> From barely speaking to each other at the beginning of rehearsals, the two groups became a cohesive company bringing laughter, joy and understanding to their audience. I think that unity between those young people will always be there and it is a state of mind that must be encouraged at every opportunity. What a vision of world peace it brings.

Peace through the Performing Arts was repeated a second year with a production of *Grimms' Fairy Tales*, but the increasing tension in Israel due to the Gaza War (December 2008 to January 2009) meant that other priorities took over and the programme with Israel stalled. Nonetheless, it was continued in South Africa with young people from the townships of Johannesburg.

Adrian reveals:

> The South African venture, like so much at the ASHA Centre, came through a connection of Zerbanoo's. She

knows everyone, everywhere. She had been very involved with the Anti-Apartheid Movement in the early eighties. Zerbanoo had been asked to present the people's petition to 10 Downing Street with Bishop Trevor Huddleston, who led the churches' fight against apartheid in South Africa. During that time, young blacks had been denied an education and it was vital for them to be given a chance to go to school. Zerbanoo's campaigning led to her being asked to say a prayer with the Nobel Prize-winning Bishop Desmond Tutu at St. Martin-in-the-Fields Church, in central London, to launch the 'Living South Africa Memorial Appeal'. Zerbanoo treasures the book that Bishop Tutu signed for her with the beautiful words: 'Thank you Zerbanoo for your help, support and prayers.'

Today she is a patron of the Bishop Simeon Trust founded by Judith Scott who has dedicated her life to the betterment of the young in South Africa. Zerbanoo is a great admirer of Judith who she feels is a modern-day Christian heroine.

Although Zerbanoo never met the late Bishop Trevor Huddleston again after that significant day at 10 Downing Street, their destinies seem to have been intertwined. She connected with another inspirational woman Tricia Sibbons, who was spearheading the Trevor Huddleston Memorial Centre in Sophiatown, Johannesburg. Inspired by his life and legacy, the centre was established in 1999 and has been running youth training and development programmes ever since.

When the ASHA Centre was unable to continue with its Israel-Palestine project, Zerbanoo contacted Tricia in South

Africa and the first of many joint theatre projects was launched in July 2008. Adrian continues:

> It is characteristic of Zerbanoo that she seeks to work with partners, believing in co-operation and sharing resources. Once she has initiated an activity, she hands it over to a trusted colleague, giving them complete freedom. I have experienced this countless times. In the case of the ongoing South African theatre projects, she had the original idea and the contact. With Zerbanoo's unswerving moral support and the immense reputation, I was given the trust and resources to run with it. I have since made several visits to the Trevor Huddleston Memorial Centre, working with groups of young South Africans from the townships, who had never before been engaged in theatre.

Groups and individuals have also visited the ASHA Centre, creating theatre productions which have toured the UK as well as South Africa. Collaborative productions include *An African Love Story, Zanandule – the Spirit of the Elephant, Othello, Sophiatown, The Crucible* and the *House of Bernarda Alba*. One of these, an *African Love Story*, about the history of their nation, was performed at St. Martin-in-the-Fields in London in May 2009 before being taken back to South Africa, where it was performed for Nelson Mandela at his home in Pretoria. Nelson Mandela enjoyed seeing himself on stage acted by Godfrey, a young man from Sophiatown who had benefitted from theatre training at the ASHA Centre.

Makhomo Tsepa, another actor from the Trevor Huddleston Memorial Centre, was on a theatre internship at the ASHA

Centre when Mandela died on 05 December 2013. In a press interview she said: 'My mother was a single parent, I had no education, but through the exchange programme with the ASHA Centre, I have found my vocation and my dream to become an actress is now coming true.'

A project close to Zerbanoo's heart is ASHA's work with orphans – especially those from Hungary, Ukraine, Armenia and Britain. For three years running, as part of the European Union funded Youth in Action programme, groups of orphans have come from these countries to the ASHA Centre and had the life-changing experience of learning the performing arts and being on stage.

Zerbanoo believes every young person needs to be loved unconditionally. For many, she is the mother they never had. She is a source of inspiration to many including Lord Karan Bilimoria who openly admits to being motivated by Zerbanoo's indomitable spirit and brave initiative in creating the ASHA Centre. As he has written: 'Zerbanoo has undoubtedly been the model for Asian youth and I for one have been a grateful recipient of this inspiration.'

Looking at the magnitude of the ASHA Foundation dream, even her well-wishers were a little concerned. They gently suggested that she learn to crawl before she could run. An actress friend advised her that she was wasting her time when she could be making a fortune in public relations, as she was the world's greatest networker. Zerbanoo ignored her advice. Her vision was that every young person needs encouragement to realize their individual gifts. At the ASHA Centre, young people are involved in non-formal education, the creative arts and sustainable living. For many, it is the first time they experience the opportunity to serve, as well as meet new friends from all over the world. It helps them realize their own potential for greatness and how good life can be.

THIRTEEN

A JEWEL IN THE FOREST

The first thing that one sees as one drives in the gates of ASHA Centre is a derelict mill nearby covered in scaffolding and sheeted in plastic covers. The mill's filthy plastic cover is torn and no one is willing to clear the mess and overgrown weeds surrounding it. It is an eyesore. The structure, listed as an 'Ancient Monument' by English Heritage, is a deceptive façade to what lies beyond.

In contrast to the dilapidated mill are the breathtakingly beautiful gardens at the ASHA Centre. A floral tapestry of thousands of roses in a burst of colours stand testimony to what an individual with single-minded purpose can achieve.

It's hard to imagine that the far end of the estate was once a junkyard. The property was completely transformed as the antique Georgian house was refurbished. The rooms were redesigned and decorated with priceless Chinese embroideries, chandeliers and English furniture from her London home.

Having been brought up in the hospitality business, Zerbanoo was aware that the ASHA Centre needed the best beds that money could buy because everybody remembers how well (or how badly) they had slept. After seeing an advertisement in the newspapers for reasonably priced orthopaedic beds, Zerbanoo travelled to Oxford Street in central London, to examine the beds. She explained to Patrick, the owner, that she wanted beds suitable for the Queen of England, but at cost price. Patrick, who would become a lifelong friend, supplied the best beds at cost price.

The damaged and unusable swimming pool at the ASHA Centre was made into a stunning glass auditorium; energy conservation systems were set up including bio-mass boilers, solar panels and solar PV panels atop the agricultural building that was the result of a grant from the Forest of Dean Local Action Group. It enabled the centre's biodynamic vegetable, herb and flower gardens to be productive throughout the year. The produce can now be dried, stored and sold through local outlets.

Zerbanoo donated fruit trees to create a Makepeace orchard to welcome the birth of her grandson, William Makepeace. Her cousin Diane generously gave hundreds of rare varieties of trees to create a fruit orchard in memory of her parents Vera and Gussie. In the years to come, the landscape will be transformed. As Zerbanoo reflects: 'Someone had the vision to plant trees for us to enjoy. We in turn plant trees for future generations to enjoy.'

The sloping wasteland beside the Georgian house was hand dug into a biodynamic fruit and vegetable garden by young volunteers from all over the world. Meals at the ASHA Centre come from the garden; it's fresh hand-picked produce grown biodynamically without fertilizers or carbon footprints. Looking at the vast estate, one would imagine that there was an army of gardeners to maintain it. When asked how he manages to maintain acres of meandering gardens, Ollie, the head gardener, laughs: 'I don't do anything. It is the angels who come at night and work on it.'

A mystical confluence of the European and Eastern comes to the fore as angel statues smile back from the nooks and corners of the estate. The merry mix of cultures against an all-encompassing garden as backdrop is a feature that characterizes ASHA. There is a pronounced oriental sense of calm as a statue of a female Bodhisattva sits calmly in the middle of the stream that runs through the gardens. The Bodhisattva is known as the 'mother of liberation' and represents the virtues of success in work and achievements, a very appropriate female role model for the Centre.

The stream that flows through ASHA springs from the sacred St. Anthony's well adjoining the land, which is visited by tourists and local people to bottle its pure water. Also, blessing the mouth of the sacred stream that flows onto the ASHA land is a figurine of the Virgin Mary in the secret garden. It is a place where many people escape to connect to the Virgin's blessings and pure power. Opposite is a Druids' grove planted with all the indigenous trees revered by ancient Britons. Within the spinney of trees is a labyrinth created on the lines of the Chartres Cathedral in France.

The mantelpiece of the very English-style sitting room at the ASHA Centre displays a set of six brass Ganeshas playing musical instruments, which Zerbanoo personally brought from India for her son, Mark. Ganesha is the Indian elephant god, widely apotheosized as the remover of obstacles, the patron of arts and sciences and the god of intellect and wisdom. Ganesha is an auspicious deity to welcome those who seek enlightenment and are looking for a fresh start in life. Like everyone else that comes to ASHA, Zerbanoo is grateful to have a new start.

Sharing a fascinating story about another serendipitous collection, she says:

> As a child, I always wanted a set of Indian clay dolls but was not allowed to have them as they were fragile and would easily break. Some years back, a local healer Pam Smee turned up at the ASHA Centre and said her grandmother, an Anglo-Indian, had given her a box of clay dolls, which she had put in her attic. She had a dream they were for me and had my name on them. She said she would bring them to me the next time she came to the ASHA Centre. True to her word, she returned with a beautiful box packed with clay dolls, which now sit on my office mantelpiece. So I did get the dolls after all. Today, they are worth a great deal of money as few people have a whole collection of all the Indian communities that make up this rare and fabulous set. They are collector's items but no one will treasure them as much as I do.

At the ASHA Centre, everyone is treasured for their uniqueness. The sound of merry laughter from one end of the emerald-green slopes comes from a diverse group of volunteers working in the vegetable garden. From a distance, it looks like they are in communion with the earth, exuding an energy that is life affirming. Volunteers work alongside students with intellectual disability from St. Christopher's School in Bristol, who visit the ASHA Centre every week. One of their long-time carers, Martin, says that working in the garden and putting their hands in the earth has a calming effect on them all. It is what the Greeks called 'kalos kai agathos' (the singular balance of the good and the beautiful).

The philosophy of Rudolf Steiner, an Austrian philosopher and social reformer, resonates at the ASHA Centre that has a long-standing relationship with the local Steiner organization, the Grange Village Camphill Community. The Grange Village, just outside Newnham on Severn on the edge of the Forest of Dean, offers an enriching life for adults with learning disabilities and other special needs. The close bond between the residents of the Grange and the volunteers at ASHA who often work together in theatre workshops and other events is inspiring and worth replicating.

ASHA was asked to run a holistic twelve-week Peace Ambassador Programme for the Grange residents. Up until then, the Grange residents thought they weren't suitable enough to be Peace Ambassadors. Zerbanoo felt otherwise and insisted that everyone should take responsibility for contributing to a peaceful world, including those with special needs. Contrary to what they thought, they were precisely the right candidates since they had no inhibitions and did what was right naturally. She would make sure they had the same training as any person who came to the ASHA Centre. The residents took great pride in being honoured as Peace Ambassadors at the completion of their course.

The unadulterated joy on their faces when the Mayor of Gloucester presented them with medals at a special ceremony was palpable. It reinforced everyone's faith in the goodness of the human spirit. It was demonstrated weeks later by Adrian Ford, a newly appointed ASHA Peace Ambassador. He stood up at their ambassadorial group reunion and revealed that he had been travelling on a bus to Gloucester when some rowdy young men began upsetting the other travellers. It was the first time he felt confident enough to stand up and say to everyone on the bus, 'I am an ASHA Peace Ambassador and I don't like the noise and aggression. Stop it now.'

To his astonishment the young men subsided and everyone applauded him.

The ASHA Centre reflects an openhearted and broadminded philosophy. Hosts of people have visited it, from anthroposophists to practitioners of yoga, Hindus, Sikhs, Buddhists, Baha'is, Jains, Zoroastrians, Muslims, Jews, Christians, Druids, native Pagans, Brahma Kumaris and followers of Sai Baba. All are made to feel welcome and a part of the wider scheme of things.

As Judy Hersch, an American IT specialist visiting the ASHA Centre for an Energy Healing course, admits:

> I can feel a sense of sacredness, a sense of belonging as I entered ASHA. You are instantly transformed and able to realize your better, higher self, because no one asks you to belong to any group and nor are you treated like a tolerated outsider. It's like coming home.

The flourishing herb garden was a gift to the Centre from Dr Kusoom Vadgama, one of ASHA's faithful trustees, to celebrate her mother Champaben's hundredth birthday. She had requested Stephen Crisp, head gardener at Winfield House (the US Ambassador's London residence), to lay out the ASHA herb garden. The plan was to host the centenarian's birthday bash in London. Later, she would inaugurate the herb garden at the ASHA Centre. Sadly, Champaben celebrated her birthday on 29 June 2009 at her home in London and then, one week later, she passed away, days before she could attend the ASHA Centre party in her honour.

Stevie Wonder, Centre manager at the ASHA Centre, remembers that Zerbanoo and he worked all night to ensure the proposed birthday party turned into a commemorative funeral.

> Zerbanoo laid out the brochure and I was told that I would no longer be Mr Wonder if I didn't get it onto the computer and printed for the next morning. Zerbanoo is a cross between a Jedi Knight, able to tap into this endless energy source and a pinball machine, bouncing from person to person, and managing to involve everyone around the world. They say Rome wasn't built in a day. It would have been if Zerbanoo was in charge. Within a matter of hours, all the leading lights from the major religions were invited to read an extract from their faith. Prince Ali Khan of Hyderabad, a patron like Zerbanoo of 'the United Religions Initiative', founded by Bishop Swing of California, read a moving piece from the Quran.

Although Champaben was a Hindu, Zerbanoo knew she would have appreciated an inter-faith funeral ceremony. A group of singers and musicians were also invited to celebrate an extraordinary life. Champaben's photograph still sits in the ASHA office as she is fondly remembered as a feminist icon from East Africa, a leading light in the early women's movement.

Steve makes it a point to mention that while his first name is Steve, his second name isn't Wonder.

> It's just that I have a knack of turning my hand to and being able to fix anything. Only Zerbanoo would've had the sense of fun to have named me Stevie Wonder. I shall never forget the look on the Marquis of Bath's face at Zerbanoo's sixtieth birthday party. I was introduced to him as Stevie Wonder and I think maybe people were expecting me to be sat at a piano, with sunglasses; singing 'Isn't She Lovely'.

As the song goes, Zerbanoo is 'wonderful' especially at connecting people and ideas. The volunteers at ASHA needed bikes to cycle to work from their beautiful Hill House home in Littledean, not far from the ASHA Centre. Without hesitation, Zerbanoo telephoned her school friend Rose Ades, who had just retired from heading the Cycling Centre of Excellence at Transport for London. Rose in turn got in touch with Mary, who sold reconditioned police bikes. All that was needed was payment. Zerbanoo wrote to Lord Tebbit for a donation. A trusted cabinet minister in Margaret Thatcher's government, he had caused controversy when he recommended that those unable to find a job should get on their bikes as his father had done during the economic recession in the 1930's, and look for employment. A week later, a cheque for the bikes arrived attached to a note from Lord Tebbit saying he felt he had been 'mugged by her'.

Winifred Baker, a documentary film-maker, was associated

with ASHA in its early stage. Talking about the infectious energy involved in working with young people she recounts,

> There were great dramas and challenges in establishing a new charity in the forest. I remember the excitement and amazing transformation in the space and the people that came to the magical place. Despite all the activity and change, building and digging, it was possible to create such a welcoming atmosphere and a sense of calmness that visitors often seemed stunned with. There was a particular look that came over their faces and you would notice a gradual relaxation of their bodies. By the time they had to leave, they were very sad to go. I think that it is quite tough to achieve a successful charity but it is even more difficult to create a truly transformational space. What Zerbanoo has achieved, in a relatively short time, is inspirational and will make a lasting impression which people like me will never forget.

Different people from all walks of life, who have been a part of the inception stage at ASHA, recall it with vivid clarity. Shirley Brown, a volunteer librarian at the Centre reminisces with relish the beautiful summer's day when,

> Zerbanoo welcomed us mature ladies from the Regency town of Cheltenham with her trademark warmth and hospitality. As we finished lunch, a van pulled up at the gates of ASHA. An Afro-Caribbean director of a charity for disadvantaged youth jumped out with a group of young men invited to stay at the Centre for a few days. The group comprised several dysfunctional youths from inner city London. They'd been in

trouble with the police and demonstrated the sullenness sadly typical of those who feel they've been betrayed by society. Jason, a mutual friend of Zerbanoo and myself, a master of Taekwondo, was also present. On noticing that the boys were getting rebellious, Jason and the charity worker-in-charge of the group decided it would be good to get the young lads to try some Taekwondo sparring.

At Zerbanoo's instigation, and at least partly due to her irrepressible sense of mischief, which I suspect she brings into play in many ways, we guests, in our best 'bibs and tuckers' trooped out to the lawn. Once we settled onto the benches, the performance began and one by one the po-faced, reluctant young men gradually began to let their defences down. There was a definite shift from a sense of defiance to the boys breaking into little grins as they were being applauded by the well-to-do ladies. The downtown boys were clearly enjoying themselves as never before, and so were the uptown ladies who hadn't experienced anything like that before. This was typical of what Zerbanoo and ASHA can do. They bring together disparate groups, cause them to meld, and the result is a dissolving of distrust and barriers, with a greater understanding of our differences; an unforgettable experience to be digested and from which to grow. The afternoon was finished off by ASHA volunteers and the young men serving us cream tea. A sight I shall never forget.

Upon discovering that Zerbanoo had donated her vast book collection to the ASHA library, Shirley offered to take on the task of reorganizing the books.

It seemed as if this discovery that ASHA library needed attention was manipulated, prised from my inner being. So began an interesting and spiritually fulfilling phase in my life. I believe that of all her many outstanding achievements in the harsh material world, Zerbanoo's founding and subsequent development of the ASHA Centre into the haven of beauty, harmony and spiritual ambience has become perhaps her greatest pride and certainly greatest joy. You become aware that you're an intricate piece of jigsaw designed to help develop the wider picture. Zerbanoo asked me to teach her the tango when she learnt I had been a ballroom dancer. She told me with a giggle that she might have to take a part in the sequel of the movie a *Scent of a Woman* and tango with Al Pacino. I taught her how to tango.

Zerbanoo's love of dancing started when she was a young girl and she would rock round the clock with her father. The ASHA Centre is a place where people are encouraged to dance. Khalid Miah, a Bangladeshi British, who studied International Relations and through a chance encounter with Zerbanoo, first volunteered and then worked for the ASHA Centre in areas of conflict management and Islamic culture. When Zerbanoo found out that Khalid was an excellent Latin dancer, she insisted that he train groups of young people to dance. Khalid remembers Zerbanoo informing him that she was going with her girlfriends to Cuba on a dance course and had to know how to Salsa in case she had to dance with Castro and his entourage. Khalid took her seriously, knowing she is capable of anything!

When I first met Zerbanoo, I thought I was meeting the Queen of England. She immediately put me at ease, and said I should continue on my path to join the British Foreign Office. Within weeks, we entertained the South Korean Ambassador and a few weeks later, the North Korean Ambassador. Zerbanoo said I should be with her as it was perfect training for my diplomatic career. Few people would allow a young person such an opportunity.

As I sat anxiously chatting with the Embassy's Cultural Attaché, I couldn't help but overhear Zerbanoo's conversation with the North Korean ambassador, informing him in her disarming yet forthright way that the imminent end of the world as predicted by the Mayan calendar would soon be upon us, 21 December 2012.

It would be a day of reckoning, or to be put it in Zerbanoo's words, 'The day when the shit hits the fan.' Although the ambassador seemed unfazed by her words, I couldn't help but feel that, had he encountered the thirty impassioned young human rights and environmental activists a few yards away in the conference room, there would've been a reckoning of some sort.

The day ended with the Ambassador asking for roses from the ASHA gardens for the embassy in London. Zerbanoo personally dug them out and presented them, saying that when she was invited to the embassy, she hoped the roses would be in full bloom. If anyone can bring the North and South Koreans together, it'll be Zerbanoo.

Everyone who visits this jewel in the forest is overwhelmed by the abundance of roses. They are also overcome by a sense of inner calm and stillness that connects with their soul. Many renowned healers feel spiritually drawn to this enchanted place where they sense a cosmic togetherness.

This magic was felt by everyone at Zerbanoo's sixtieth birthday, which marked the official opening of the ASHA Centre. It was also the turning point in modern British politics. 11 May 2010 was the day that the Conservatives and the Liberal Democrat parties joined in a coalition to run Britain for the next five years. The Centre was inaugurated by the quintessentially English and colourful personality, the Marquis of Bath. The Bishop of Tewkesbury, unveiled the Celtic cross created as a special gift by sculptor, David Lovemore, for Zerbanoo's birthday. The three hundred special invitees included royalty, diplomats, politicians, inter-faith leaders, Hollywood producers and media moguls, who walked towards the Peace Grove where leaders of different faiths offered their prayers and blessings together while they each planted a tree representing their faith. Everyone present could feel the powerful vibrations of the prayers chanted. British Zoroastrian High Priest, Rusi Bhedwar, offered bundles of wood to the dancing flames in the huge fire pit. After all the rituals, prayers and blessings, a former Jain monk, editor and nominee for the Nobel Peace Prize, Satish Kumar, declared the Golden Tiger Eco Lodge, built especially for Zerbanoo's birthday, open.

The entertainment that followed was equally captivating. Caroline Liljestrom Marcus, a Swedish Eurythmist, orchestrated a beautiful sequence for Zerbanoo. Eurythmy is a spiritual and artistic art form of expression introduced by Rudolf Steiner. Caroline had choreographed an ethereal dance involving twelve friends dressed up in robes to represent the qualities of the planets at the moment of her birth. The aesthetically performed rendition captured Zerbanoo's courage and joie de vivre.

Vedic astrology predicts that the future according to Zerbanoo's chart is groundbreaking; her life work has just begun. By the time she reaches her late sixties, she'll step into her 'sun period'. Everything will then come to fruition. She has put the foundations in place to achieve her 'atma' (roughly translated as life purpose). She will be a key player in the international arena, shaping a new world for the young.

Tariq Qureishy, Founder of 100 per cent Make A Difference (MAD), who lives in Dubai and is also dedicated to empowering the young, recalls meeting Zerbanoo at an awards party in Henley on Thames.

We instantly hit it off because we are both intuitive and passionate about changing the world. Zerbanoo moves very fast and has clarity of thought. She's spontaneous, authentic and impatient, already two steps ahead of her game. She breaks paradigms, is tenacious and has a clear focus of where she is going. Intuition is advanced intelligence. It's when the conscious and subconscious work together to give you the answers. Zerbanoo is rapidly intuitive. Thousands of young people who have been to the ASHA Centre take away a new sense of themselves and the confidence to change their world. No one doubts that in the future there will be ASHA Centres everywhere in the world.

FOURTEEN

SPIRITUAL WARRIOR

The prime focus of Zoroastrianism, the early Iranian religion founded by Prophet Zarathustra, is essentially on the good mind known as the Vahu Manu. Only if you have a good mind, will good thoughts, words and deeds follow. The onus lies on every individual having the freedom to make the moral choice between just and unjust acts in order to follow the path of *Asha*, meaning righteousness and hope.

The ancient scriptures talk about truth, not just in terms of falsehood, but in actively creating an ideal world and living in harmony with mankind and nature.

Zerbanoo takes pride in belonging to a long line of humanitarians who changed the course of history. The Persian king, Cyrus the Great, known as the father of human rights, was the first ruler to be given the title 'the Great'. He ruled the largest empire known to the ancient world and yet gave all the people in his kingdom freedom to follow their own religion. He knew tolerance would lead to peace.

Cyrus the Great is the only foreign leader to be conferred

the title of the King of Kings, God's anointed in the Bible. His memory is immortalized as the Persian king who not only released the Jews from their captivity in Babylon but also helped them rebuild their temple in Jerusalem around 538 BC. The east door of the temple had a picture of the Persian capital city of Susa to remind the Jewish worshippers of their Iranian saviour. Today, Cyrus the Great's decree is recognized as the world's first human rights declaration and preserved in a clay cylinder at the British Museum in London. Translated in all six official UN languages, a replica of the cylinder is also at the United Nations' Headquarters in New York City.

Cyrus the Great is one of Zerbanoo's favourite heroes.

He set free the Jewish slaves and empowered them to go back to their own country and to flourish. He didn't try to impose his Zoroastrian religion on them or subject them to servitude. I think it is fair to say that Zoroastrianism was the first religion to propagate the idea of one God, the need to live a good life and that there will be a day of reckoning. The oldest monotheistic religion has played a central role in influencing Buddhism and the Abrahamic religions of Judaism, Christianity and Islam. The genius of Prophet Zarathustra is that his religious revelations have become the core of many of the world's major religions.

Our religion has given the world an understanding of the hierarchy of angels and other beings that support us during this life. The concept of the Messiah is rooted in Zoroastrianism. But what really appeals to me about my faith is that you hold your destiny in your own hands. Our religion is not about suffering or renunciation but about having a

good life and giving others a good time. At the end of the
day, you are responsible for your thoughts and words and are
accountable for your actions. Heaven and Hell are not just
places you go to but different states of awareness that you
experience. In order to touch a higher state of consciousness
you have to learn to grow up spiritually and be in harmony
with the cosmos. Zoroastrianism has been hailed as the
first green religion that condemns the pollution of nature.
Zoroastrians are not allowed to pollute the elements, be it in
life or death.

No one knows the exact date when Zoroastrianism was born,
but it was probably around four millennia ago. Legend has it
that the three wise men were enlightened Zoroastrian priests
(Magi) with great knowledge of astronomy and astrology. Upon
seeing the Star of Splendour, they followed it to the nativity in
Bethlehem. The wise men knew that a great soul had arrived to
save mankind and carried gifts of gold, frankincense and myrrh
for baby Jesus. Zoroastrianism went on to be the state religion
of the Achaemenid, Parthian and Sassanian Empires of Persia.

The followers of the religion were persecuted after the
invaders conquered Persia in the seventh century. They were
cruelly coerced to convert and those who resisted were harassed
incessantly. It was the death knell for practising Zoroastrians as
they were publicly discriminated against. The devout followers
of the religion were subjected to humiliation, heavy taxes and
lopsided inheritance laws. Their homes and Fire Temples were
violated. Zoroastrian horseback riders, known the world over
for their riding skills, were forced to ride donkeys and banned

from entering the marketplace. To add insult to injury, the donkey was permitted to go through a public square, whereas its Zoroastrian owner was not allowed to do so.

Making life hell for them were tax collectors. They would ruthlessly rip off the sacred thread that Zoroastrians wore around their waist as a sign of the holy triad of good thoughts, words and deeds. The tax collectors would shame them by hanging the sacred chord around the necks of the beleaguered followers of the Zoroastrian faith. However, in spite of being driven to the depths of despair, the diehard Zoroastrians only grew all the more determined to hold on to their way of living and belief system. The subconscious memories of the oppression remains embedded in the collective DNA of the Zoroastrians. Zerbanoo believes it may be the trigger that pushes her to fight for the underdog and those persecuted for their beliefs.

Her grandfather, Shapoor Mazda, left Iran and spent four years walking to India to escape religious persecution in the country where he was born. He would often regale Zerbanoo with stories of the time when no Zoroastrians, Jews or Armenian Christians could go outside when it rained. The blessed rain didn't fall on nonbelievers. If they touched the food it was instantly thrown away as it was considered unclean. He would watch his mother make clothes from scraps of cloth because Zoroastrians in those days were not allowed to buy material from the shops. Their clothes were made up of patchwork so that they could be identifiable in a crowd. This is something that probably stayed with Zerbanoo, given her passion for collecting old discarded pieces of material and artfully weaving them together to create unique outfits. As a young mother, she would spend her evenings watching television making patchwork quilts using every inch of material discarded by others.

Zerbanoo's favourite story is about the arrival of the Zoroastrians over a thousand years ago on the shores of Western India. A group of Zoroastrians fled Persia in search of a new home where they could continue practising their faith without being persecuted. A small contingent crossed the rough seas to arrive by boat at the shores of Sanjan in Gujarat. They requested the Hindu raja, Jadav Rana to allow them to settle on Indian soil. The king was hesitant. He called for a bowl of milk and filled it to the brim to illustrate to the foreigners that his country was overpopulated and could not receive any more immigrants.

The Zoroastrian head priest thought and acted quickly. He called for some sugar and carefully dissolved it in the bowl of milk. He had demonstrated without words that the Zoroastrians would be like the sugar – they would integrate and sweeten their new homeland, and not displace the milk in the bowl or inconvenience the already existing populace.

The Raja was so impressed that he agreed to welcome the exhausted refugees on certain conditions: they would not indulge in missionary activities; they would dress like the locals; speak the local language, Gujarati; perform their wedding ceremonies after sunset; never bear arms against their Hindu neighbours and would peacefully co-exist and integrate into the Indian fabric.

A promise the Parsis (people from Pars) have kept to this day. They have enriched India in every field of endeavour and have never converted anybody to their religion.

In gratitude, Zerbanoo in her speeches and writing always makes it a point to mention this story and the wisdom of the Gujarati king. She professes that refugees should be welcomed but there should also be guidelines for them to follow, including learning the local language so that they can contribute to every aspect of their new homeland.

Zerbanoo's own ancestors remained in Iran around the village of Yazd, until the beginning of the twentieth century, when they migrated to India in search of a new life. They were called Irani, because they came from Iran, the modern name for ancient Persia. They hoped their co-religionists, the successful Parsis (people who came from Persia), who had left Iran and settled in India a millennium ago, would befriend them.

Today, with less than a hundred thousand Zoroastrians left in the world, Zerbanoo can't resist comparing them to an endangered species like the pandas. She jokingly says she is surprised the Worldwide Wildlife Fund has still not put a preservation order on Zoroastrians. Time and again, Zerbanoo has striven to bring to the attention of a wider audience the lives of outstanding Zoroastrian men and women worldwide.

The Z-factor exhibition in 2012, was held to mark the thirtieth anniversary of Zerbanoo's election and to highlight exceptional Zoroastrians worldwide. The scroll of honour was both impressive and exhaustive. Men who changed the world they lived in like Dadabhai Naoroji, Britain's first Asian MP; Shapurji Saklatvala, the sole communist MP in the British House of Commons in the twenties; and Sam Manekshaw, India's first field marshal, made their presence felt. Adorning the panels of the exhibit was the first Indian baronet, Sir

Jamshedji Jeejeebhoy. He started life washing and selling bottles and rose to create an extraordinary business empire. He contributed generously in the mid-nineteenth century to relief efforts for the famine in Ireland, the floods in France and the fires in Bombay and Surat in India, apart from building educational and art institutes and hospitals.

In an attempt to inspire people, Zerbanoo showcased the lives of other philanthropic greats like Jamshedji Tata, the founder of the Tata Group, India's conglomerate and the leading manufacturing employer in India and Britain today; and his heirs JRD Tata, the founder of Air India, and more recently Ratan Tata, who has led the Tatas to an extraordinary international status. Lowjee Nusserwanjee Wadia, master shipbuilder responsible for building many of the British navy's ships including, HMS Cornwallis, on which Wadia, in 1800 AD, had defiantly carved: 'This ship was built by a damned black fellow'.

It was his way of protesting against the racism of some officers in the Royal Navy in those days.

The exhibition paid homage to other leading Zoroastrians who contributed with their imagination, integrity and industry to build the metropolitan cities of Mumbai, Karachi, Aden and Hong Kong.

Other megastars featured were Freddie Mercury, born Farrokh Bulsara in Zanzibar, the rock legend and lead singer of the band Queen, whose song *We are the Champions* was voted 'Song of the Millennium'; one of the world's best known conductors, Zubin Mehta, the music director for *Life for the Israeli Philharmonic Orchestra*; Cyrus Poonawalla the vaccine king and chairman of Poonawalla Group, which includes the privately owned Serum Institute of India, India's top biotech company and the world's largest vaccine manufacturer; Meher Baba, born Merwan Sheriar Irani, a mystic, spiritual master and an acclaimed avatar with a worldwide following, and the inspiration for the song *Don't Worry, Be Happy*.

Among the women who stood tall was Madame Bhikaji Cama, a fiery Indian revolutionary at the heart of the Indian Independence movement. Other iconic women with grit and character were: Cornelia Sorabji, the first female graduate from Poona University and the first woman to read law at Oxford University; Avabai Wadia, founder of the International Planned Parenthood Federation who led the campaign for the right to birth control in India and across the globe; Art connoisseur, author and founder of the Cymroza Art Gallery, Pheroza Godrej, known for promoting young artists and bringing Indian art to the world stage; Maja Daruwala, head of the Commonwealth Human Rights Initiative and Coomi Kapoor, president of the Indian Women's Press Association.

The Z-factor paid tribute to numerous Zoroastrian women imbued with a pioneering spirit and the drive for freedom and gender equality.

However, the fate of the community that has made giant strides in every field of endeavour, today hangs by a fine thread between the opposing poles of orthodoxy and progressiveness. Endless debates on mixed marriages and the exclusion of the children of Zoroastrian mothers has divided the peace-loving community into bitter factions.

In a world ravaged by religious fanaticism, the Zoroastrians stand out as the only race that zealously guards its ethnic, cultural and religious identity with such fierce pride that it refuses to convert people into its fold.

Disappointed with the stance the orthodox keepers of the religion have taken, whereby they allow men to marry non-Zoroastrian women and bring them and their children into the fold but the same courtesy is not extended to women, Zerbanoo openly questions the lack of gender equality.

> The Zoroastrian religion empowers women. Our Prophet Zarathustra said that each person has to decide with their own conscience between right and wrong. Men and women have free will. He perceived men and women as equals. Up to then, in the ancient world, women weren't valued. He challenged that. Unfortunately, today, the religion is being taken over by a few who have misinterpreted his high ideas and have used their power to exclude women. Nothing about women being second-class citizens is mentioned in our holy scriptures. No religious charlatan with his hogwash interpretations of our beautiful religion can stop me from being a Zoroastrian. So what if I married an Englishman?
>
> Zoroastrian men are allowed to marry anybody and their children can be brought up as Zoroastrians. Why should a woman who marries outside her community be prevented from welcoming her children into her faith? My sons know our prayers better than I do, but are too respectful to ever force their way into our Fire Temples or to challenge the self-appointed guardians of our noble religion. It saddens me to think that they cannot be welcomed into a faith that is so much part of me, especially since my sons know so much more about the religion than most Zoroastrians do. How can

anyone discriminate against another and think they are true Zoroastrians?

She further reasons saying it is a woman who gives birth to a child and only she knows who the father is.

As they say, it's a lucky man who knows his children. In the Jewish faith, they have the wisdom to realize it is only the mother who knows the child's father. It is the mother who cares for the child and initiates the child into its religious observances. The faith goes through her.

We sometimes forget that no religion grows in splendid isolation. Religions continue to interact, influence, cross-fertilize, assimilate and transform within their own traditions. For someone like me, who is so involved in the inter-faith movement and the need to understand others faiths, the enemy is not religious difference, or inter-religious differences but indifference to God.

I believe that we come from God and return to God and the interlude in between needs to be lived magnificently. There is no doubt I am a Zoroastrian, but I am also attracted to the great Hindu scriptures that acknowledge the supreme reality that you have always existed and will always exist. I also appreciate the Hindu concept that the final stages of your life should be spent in thoughtful retreat in the forest. You have lived your life, had a family and a career and then it's time to reflect and prepare to leave this existence. I'm living in my final forest period now, and it's wonderful. My life has revolved around action: taking the world on and confronting evil in its many ugly forms; beautifying and cherishing our environment; and just adoring those with whom we are privileged to spend time. I have been so fortunate to have experienced angels and God's grace, knowing from a young age what was expected of me. But I have also learnt to be less firm with myself. As my mother always tells me, 'The day will come and the day will go.' It puts it all into perspective. I hope all God expects is for us to be kind to ourselves, other people, and the natural world until we rejoin Him.

Until then, Zerbanoo spiritedly continues in her quest of giving without expecting any returns. She quotes the Sufi mystic Hafiz saying: 'Even after all this time, the sun never says to the earth, "You owe me." Look what happens with a love like that. It lights the whole sky.'

FIFTEEN

SAINTS AND SEERS

Building relationships whilst actively seeking and exploring novel situations is the core determinant that differentiates a curious mind from one that prefers being strapped to a safety net.

A fleeting encounter at the airport or 40,000 feet above sea level in a plane, is all it takes her curious mind to be drawn to people of interest. On a flight to Bangalore, India, Zerbanoo was feeling uneasy and got up to make her way to the washroom. While walking through the aisle, she tripped on a beautifully carved walking stick. Far from getting annoyed, she saw it as a perfect excuse to strike up a conversation with the elderly mistress of the stick. The regal-looking lady was Phyllis Krystal, a spiritual giantess and a lifelong devotee of the avatar Sathya Sai Baba. Phyllis works with the inner wisdom, the higher consciousness. They bonded instantly.

Extremely fond of the spiritual psychotherapist with whom she shares her birthday, Zerbanoo hosted a grand ninety-fifth birthday party for her at the ASHA Centre and recently celebrated Phyllis's 101st birthday quietly with her at her home in England.

When Zerbanoo and Phyllis were in Puttaparthi, visiting the avatar Sathya Sai Baba's Ashram in south India, Phyllis sensed a blockage in Zerbanoo's stomach and later conducted psychic surgery on her, a new experience which she valued.

Some years later, sipping a cup of hot water at a local hotel in Hardwar, overlooking the River Ganges in India, Zerbanoo's curiosity was piqued by a glorious figure in orange robes surrounded by an entourage. Knowing that she had some time on hand before boarding the night train to Delhi, Zerbanoo walked up to the woman in saffron regalia and introduced herself saying she was just 'going with the flow'.

She must have uttered the magic words because Swamini Kaliji beamed with delight saying, 'going with the flow' was her secret mantra. There was an instant connection with the yogini, the internationally acclaimed founder of Triyoga, an arm of an ancient tradition that integrates Eastern thought with Western tradition. The Californian Yogi, who taught Triyoga for over forty years, spoke with finger mudras (yoga of the hands), spontaneously linking and interlinking them. The outcome of the fleeting encounter was a lasting one as Kaliji later held master classes in Triyoga at the ASHA Centre. She is now Zerbanoo's grandson William Makepeace's spiritual grandmother.

Most mortals strive to live their lives with the hope of becoming a beautiful memory in the hearts of others. Mother Theresa, whose memory lives on in millions of hearts, left Zerbanoo a special prayer to remember her by. Those were chaotic days when Zerbanoo was making a Channel 5 television documentary on the lives of street children. In between juggling a hundred other responsibilities, she fixed an appointment with Mother Theresa to seek her blessings for the new ASHA project to take off.

The arranged meeting in Kolkata never happened due to Mother Theresa's ill health that kept her back in Rome where she was visiting Pope John Paul II. However, upon her return to India, Mother Theresa wrote a touching prayer for Zerbanoo. Coincidentally, in the week that Princess Diana's shocking death made global headlines, Zerbanoo was making a national appeal for street children on British television. Mother Theresa died in the same week in the month of August 1997. Zerbanoo used the occasion to read her prayer on television. The much-treasured prayer now has a pride of place at the ASHA Centre.

It is now acknowledged that in order to attract positive people and things into our lives we need to actively seek new experiences that the universe willingly orchestrates. Quantum Physics has proved that each person is a bubbling vortex of energy with different vibrational frequencies that help draw like-minded people to them. Zerbanoo has undoubtedly been able to harness that power. In turn she has been blessed and guided by many of the world's spiritual leaders.

Zerbanoo must have fine-tuned that power to have been chosen for a personal meeting with His Holiness Pope John Paul II. While many across the globe wait endlessly for a one-on-one with His Holiness, Zerbanoo received his blessings for the ASHA Centre. Draped in a black lace veil gifted to her by members of the Polish community, she could feel the Pope's powerful aura even though he was old and frail, sitting nearly motionless on his throne in the Vatican.

In the brief exchange the Pope had with Zerbanoo on the idea behind ASHA, Zerbanoo was informed that His Holiness had launched his own committee for justice. He told her that he fully supported what she was trying to do and what he described as the first World Peace Centre for the young, stated the *Harrow Times*.

However, the newspaper missed out on the baffled expression on the Pope's face when Zerbanoo softly whispered 'Bless you' as their meeting was drawing to a close. It was her way of saying 'thank you' but the Pope was confused. The Swiss guards standing by watching every micro expression on the Pope's face immediately leaped forward to protect the Pope to check if there was a security threat. It was a comical moment. Zerbanoo puts it down to a misunderstanding of the subtleties of the English language saying the Pope probably wasn't expecting to be blessed by those who come to seek his blessings.

Drawn towards extraordinary beings, Zerbanoo's spiritual encounters with enlightened souls have been turning points in her life.

Amongst her many paranormal experiences was one when she and her son Mark attended a spiritual gathering hosted by Almine the Countess of Shannon, a shaman. Almine had sensed Zerbanoo's lack of faith. She announced that everyone present would hold hands and use the power of the collective mind. It was a sunny day in England but they would call for rain in Kent. The group present went into deep meditation. Surprisingly they experienced thunder, lightning and rain for a few minutes. The small village in Kent was the only place in Britain that experienced rainfall that day.

In 2001, Zerbanoo was one of the few women invited to New York to attend the United Nations Millennium conference of spiritual leaders. Taking the opportunity to meet so many evolved souls in one place, she asked Alexander who had just come down from Oxford to join her for the once-in-a-lifetime experience. At the venue, one of India's leading industrialists, Dr B.K. Modi, introduced her to a host of spiritual giants attending the conference. It was here that she re-met Swami Muni Ji whom she and Alexander had met previously at his ashram in Rishikesh and had the privilege to receive spiritual nurturing. The honour of being asked by him to begin the evening aarti by the River Ganges was a beautiful memory embedded in her heart.

At the New York UN conference, Alexander and Zerbanoo spent time with the charismatic Sufi leader, Pir Vilayat Khan, brother of the Second World War heroine, Noor Inayat Khan. Vilayat blessed Alexander and said that he had instantly recognized that Alexander was to bring the story of his courageous sister Noor, codenamed Madeleine, to global audiences. He would be happy if Alexander wrote the script about his extraordinary sister's life and death in the Dachau concentration camp and capture it on celluloid.

Throughout Zerbanoo's life, the many setbacks she has suffered have actually been a process of clearing the way for her life's foreordained task. She has allowed herself to be open to the universe and in turn, there has been a steady flow of higher souls assisting in her spiritual growth.

She admits she didn't know much about the avatar Sathya Sai Baba until a Gujarati colleague and an ardent devotee requested her to make a trip to Puttaparthi, near Bangalore city, India.

He told her that Baba had called for her and would change her life as he had done for millions of people around the world.

Zerbanoo made her first trip to Puttaparthi, with her son Mark, during that tumultuous phase in her life when she had left no stone unturned to create the ASHA Centre. Her meeting with Sai Baba was a singular moment in her life. Millions of his devotees from 126 countries had received darshan from him, but few had been summoned for a series of private audiences with him.

> Sai Baba told me he wanted me to continue empowering women and children and that women would be soon taking their rightful place in the world. He then blessed the ASHA project and assured me that things would fall into place. When I asked him where the money and the premises would come from, he waved his arms and said, 'What is ten pounds or ten million pounds? Be assured you will have the ASHA Centre.'

Then the spiritual guru took some vibhuti (sacred ash) and blew it over Zerbanoo. He offered to materialize two rings for her. To which Zerbanoo answered: 'It would be a bit greedy to ask for two rings. I would love to have one, thank you.'

Sai Baba seemed impressed as he sagely observed, 'Not a greedy bone in your body,' and then materialized a special ring for her.

> Whenever I really want some help, I look at the ring and somehow my wishes, if they are good for me, are granted. I usually ask Baba to have me upgraded on planes as I hate

flying. I am sure he is tired of my travel requests. He is probably smiling and thinking, 'I wish she would just stay at home.'

The second time she visited Puttaparthi, Zerbanoo was accompanied by her younger son, Alexander and her aunt, Mappie. Once again, she was invited for a private audience, along with Alexander. Grateful for the opportunity, Zerbanoo quickly pushed her aunt Mappie in front of her into the audience room since she knew that Mappie was eager to receive Baba's blessings, although she had not been called for an interview.

Upon seeing Mappie, Sai Baba asked Zerbanoo who she was.

'You should know. If you don't know, who does? You know everything. She is Air Marshal Dhatigara's wife,'

Sai Baba was amused by Zerbanoo's cheeky repartee to the question. She says, 'I think Baba liked fun people. Poor Mappie couldn't sit cross-legged on the floor due to her arthritic knees. Seeing how uncomfortable she was, Sai Baba stood up and called for a chair for her. He was extremely perceptive and knew everything, especially what was in your heart.'

Alexander recalls Baba saying that, 'Mother is divine.' He's not sure if that meant his mother or all mothers. Nonetheless, he is sure Baba loved his mother for her extreme generosity.

My mother gives abundantly and is, therefore, loved by many people. She believes in the Zoroastrian doctrine of the 'good fight' and feels strongly directed to positively transform the earth. All this has come together beautifully at the ASHA Centre: a place of great generosity, where both, the souls of people and the soil of the earth are creatively enriched. Here, I feel my mother's own nature and soul purpose is fulfilled

in full measure. Baba knew that and helped make the ASHA
Centre a reality.

Zerbanoo believes there was divine intervention in the court
battle over the land that she had brought legally in Harrow
for the proposed ASHA site. It had been years of hard work
and frustration that led up to the court case to prove her legal
entitlement to the land.

We had spent the whole week in the High Court, knowing
that our integrity and the creation of the ASHA Centre were
at stake. It was on a Thursday, which is Sai Baba's special day,
and I think I saw him sitting next to Judge Lord Neuberger.
I remember how tired I was. I wasn't sure I was imagining it
but I did say to myself, 'I've had enough; put a stop to this
nonsense. We need to win this case and keep the land we have
legally bought if we are to fulfil our mission.' Then a most
extraordinary thing happened, the government's legal team
threw their hand in. I have never been able to tell the whole
story as we were made to undertake a court order not to
divulge what happened that day. Obviously, it was to protect
the government. We did win the legal case and I am in no
doubt that the higher forces played their part. Without their
help, nothing good would have been possible. Throughout my
life, I have been blessed with the most extraordinary grace. I
know how fortunate I am.

SIXTEEN

COSMIC NETWORKER

As a five-year-old, Zerbanoo sat up all night to see what Father Christmas looked like when he dropped down the chimney. Nothing would make her go to bed until she caught a glimpse of Santa Claus. Finally, her parents had no option but to leave her Christmas stocking full of gifts in the outside toilet. The best explanation they could come up with was that Father Christmas had to take a different route since the chimney was blocked. That really upset Zerbanoo because she wanted to talk to Santa and thank him personally for his generosity.

Last Christmas, her mother Kitty, whilst trying to help her daughter with writing well over two thousand Christmas cards, threw up her hands. She thought it was just too much work for a ninety-year-old to keep up with her daughter's ever-expanding list of friends.

In a world that tweets and tags, with the illusion of having thousands of friends (but sadly none who can be relied upon), Zerbanoo has a directory of loyal friends she can call on anytime of the day or night. It's her unlimited capacity to nurture and invest time and energy that results in long-lasting friendships all over the world. A seasoned journalist once labelled her a 'cosmic networker', and not without reason. Chatting with Professor Gerard Bodeker whilst waiting for a taxi at the Frankfurt Airport, she discovered they were both heading to the same International Maharishi Yogi conference in Bonn, Germany. At the conference, Zerbanoo won over seasoned scientists with her inimitable style of delivery and received a standing ovation from the intelligentsia. Although they were mostly interested in the way the mind expanded with meditation techniques, Zerbanoo's uncensored talk had them listening with rapt attention.

After the conference, whilst exchanging visiting cards, Zerbanoo once again found herself talking to Professor Bodeker, senior clinical lecturer in public health at the Oxford Medical School. Fascinated by the research he was doing with herbs, she spontaneously agreed to accompany him on his next trip to the foothills of the Himalayas. Zerbanoo, her son Alexander and journalist friend Fionnuala McHugh packed their bags to make their way to Rishikesh where they caught up with Dr Bodeker in the holy land of pilgrims.

Much as Zerbanoo's life experiences make interesting narratives, there are those few and far between moments when she is forced to listen with her mouth wide open. Those, of course, only occur when she is at the dentist. Dr Giovanni Dicran Megighian first came across Zerbanoo at his friend Dr Parag Patel's dental surgery in Harley Street, London where he was a visiting consultant. It was then that a 'grande amitié' developed and blossomed. The three words he uses to describe Zerbanoo are perception, compassion and acceptance. 'If I had to describe the beat of her soul, I would use the tempo "allegro ma non troppo, un poco maestoso",' like the first movement of Beethoven's ninth symphony, prelude to the *Ode to Joy*.

Dr Giovanni recalls an episode that cheers him up when he revisits his days of darkness. He backtracks to their trip through India, to describe a scenario of the two of them waiting for a domestic flight in the dilapidated departure lounge of an aerodrome. While he was trying to kill time at the airport by playing a game of solitaire on his laptop, Zerbanoo was trying in vain to find a comfortable position on the plastic and once chrome-plated seat.

> She asked, 'What are you doing?' I said, 'I am playing solitaire.' To which Zerbanoo retorted, 'Nonsense! You should go and conquer the world. And, by the way, can you get me a cup of "garam pani" on the way?' I dutifully went in search of hot water and as I passed the airport bookstall there was her latest book *Confessions to a Serial Womaniser* staring at me.

That was a double impact as he had not one but two Zerbanoos looking back at him, one from the bookstand and the other waiting in person for a glass of hot water.

When she is not daring her friends to go out and conquer the world, Zerbanoo indulges in her favourite pastime of connecting like-minded people. The British Indian food writer and television presenter, Karen Anand believes Zerbanoo's introductions lead to strong, sometimes inexplicable friendships. Zerbanoo introduced Dr Giovanni to Karen while they were all unexpectedly on the Cote D'Azur.

There was a cosmic hand at work. Giovanni helped us source the best olive oil in the world. His Italian girlfriend owned a jam business in Italy as did we in India. My husband, Yadu, and I became close to him in a very strange way, as if we had known Giovanni for years and in some other life, and our lives are linked on many levels. Zerbanoo creates combinations that allow people to ignite lasting friendships and fulfil deeply buried dreams.

Historian Dr Kusoom Vadgama was keen to organize the centenary celebration of the first Indian Member of British Parliament, Dadabhai Naoroji. She gives Zerbanoo credit for helping her realize her long-standing dream. Zerbanoo's extraordinary connections made a spate of celebratory events a reality in 1992.

They included a gala dinner at the House of Commons, a gathering at the Ismaili Centre in Kensington, with Lord Steel as chief guest and the launch of Zerbanoo's book on Dadabhai Naoroji, at the inaugural opening of the Nehru Centre in London. The late Nani Palkhivala, India's renowned jurist and ambassador to the US, was the guest of honour.

Connie Jackson, an African American, remembers how she was impressed with the spontaneously generous way Zerbanoo worked when she first met her at a private dinner for the Canadian prime minister, Kim Campbell, at the House of Lords. A trailblazer in her own right, Connie had arrived from America to start a job as Chief Executive of the Bartholomew and London Hospital and was interested in making inroads into the Bangladeshi community in East London. Zerbanoo immediately agreed to set up a dinner at the famous Cinnamon Club in Westminster to connect Connie to those she needed to meet in London. Connie says, 'I was introduced to Rifat Wahhab, a strategic health facilitator and her brother Iqbal, the owner of the club, and subsequently met all the relevant people.'

Diana Maclellan has watched Zerbanoo from the sidelines as she moved heaven and earth to make the ASHA Centre a reality. When Zerbanoo asked if she would hold a workshop for the Lila Fellows at the Centre, the trainer and practitioner of the Alexander Technique and NLP (Neuro Linguistic Programming) was more than happy to offer her skills. Zerbanoo felt the girls needed confidence-building exercises that would eventually help them position themselves for interviews and other personal interactions.

Diana believes Zerbanoo has a positive placebo effect on people as she releases their handbrakes and makes them feel they can put their foot down and drive in the fast lane. She raises their vibrations and makes them feel good about themselves. A witness to the dramatic transformation in underprivileged girls from India, Diana enthuses, 'The girls were so shy, yet after a close interaction with Zerbanoo they were far more confident and empowered.'

When the workshops were wrapped up, Zerbanoo and Diana took off on a memorable holiday to Venice and enjoyed admiring the many wonders in the Gondola city during a private tour of St. Lazarus, the island that was given to the Armenians in the eighteenth century. They were greeted by the monks at the Armenian Church and shown the wonderful Armenian museum on the island. St. Lazarus Island, they discovered, was where the flamboyant and notorious English poet, Lord Byron, used to swim to while on his creative escapades. Diana remembers Zerbanoo wooing the two resident monks with her love and knowledge of the Armenian community. Summing up her experience in the city where they spent so much time searching for the perfect pair of blue suede shoes to match Zerbanoo's embroidered Kashmiri coat, she says, 'Venice was perfect the backdrop to welcome a beautiful modern-day Renaissance woman.'

For someone who hates travelling, it is difficult to comprehend why Zerbanoo plans a trip while she is already undertaking another one. The only explanation could be that although she has inherited her mother's motion sickness, she is also driven by the wanderlust bequeathed by her father. As she says, 'Wherever I travel I inevitably end up sitting next to fascinating people. I start a conversation and the magic begins. I couldn't agree more with the visionary Rudolph Steiner when he said, "To know about the world look deeply within your own being. To know about yourself meet the world."'

During her early twenties, Zerbanoo was one of the few adventurous people to step out of her comfort zone and travel to China at the end of the Chinese Cultural Revolution. That period was conflict-ridden; most people used their better judgment and refrained from venturing out, however, the mystical pull to China couldn't be denied. Her sixth sense tells her she has spent several lifetimes there and that explains her fascination with the country, its people and especially its antique embroidery. The wall-to-wall frames at her home, as well as the ASHA Centre displaying the exquisite art of Chinese embroidery stand testimony to her deep-rooted enthrallment for the dying art.

In hindsight, as Zerbanoo recalls the Trans-Siberian Rail journey she undertook as a young girl, she is puzzled by her father's incongruity. On the one hand, Bailey had always declared a curfew and insisted that she be home before the pubs closed at 11 o'clock (although the young and rebellious Zerbanoo would argue that even Cinderella could stay out until midnight); and on the other hand, he had encouraged her to take the longest rail journey in the world, spanning two continents and across nearly a third of the globe.

> Strangely, he never allowed me to go on a train from London to Brighton by myself in case I got assaulted, but he was not worried about me travelling through South America in the footsteps of the crazed Conquistadors. I passed out whilst crossing the high altitudes of the Andes on a train and needed oxygen to be revived. I thought I must be bonkers to go through all that. But I suppose we should be allowed some madness otherwise life would be so predictable.

People also thought she was crazy when she came up with the idea of interviewing three hundred women from across sixty countries for a book titled *Confessions to a Serial Womaniser*. She dwells on the ignition that fired her with the idea:

> It was Tagore's poem contrasting the butterfly to the humble bee that has originally inspired me on my quest. I had given

myself the challenge to see whether I could be like the useful bee that spontaneously carried pollen from flower to flower, thereby setting the whole landscape alight with colour and fragrance rather than the vain butterfly that fluttered around thinking she was beautiful but actually doing nothing.

Although it seemed like an improbable idea initially, she eventually succeeded in collating the personal life experiences of the twenty-first-century women achievers. Exhausted yet driven, she met some of the most remarkable women alive and learnt from them that often the secret to worldly success is hard work, being adaptable and taking one's opportunities when they appear.

Interestingly, two of the seven books that Zerbanoo authored, *The Golden Thread – Asian Experiences in Post-Raj Britain* and the *Confessions to a Serial Womaniser: Secrets of the World's Inspirational Women* have a biographical base, capturing the inexorable strength and varied experiences of iconoclastic women. Her penchant for covering such a vast array of global leading lights speaks volumes of her innate curiosity to get to know the silent desires, hopes and reflections of women perceived as powerful and inspiring.

It was her intrinsic desire to be surrounded by women of substance with lofty ideals that made her spontaneously contact a dynamic woman she saw on the BBC news one morning. Hearing Frene Ginwala, head of the African National Congress (ANC) in London and the first woman speaker of the National Assembly of South Africa, talk, Zerbanoo did not waste any time. She immediately rang the lady for an interview and included Frene in her book on outstanding Asian women. It was through Frene Ginwala that Zerbanoo was introduced to Govan Mbeki, the revolutionary leader of the ANC who was in prison with Nelson Mandela. The memorable meeting with the iconic hero instrumental in writing modern history, stayed with Zerbanoo forever.

> I asked Govan Mbeki, the father of Thabo Mbeki, the second president of South Africa, how he and Mandela had survived twenty-seven years in prison. Mbeki said that it was so cold on Robben Island that they would have to exercise for at least an hour to get warm enough to sleep. Their meals were just a bowl of porridge. On the twelfth year of imprisonment, as a treat for his birthday, he was given a slice of bread. I wrote an article after this meeting entitled: 'Man doesn't live by bread alone.'

A fascination to meet those who wielded power as heads of government and shaped nations, led Zerbanoo to fix an appointment with the first woman prime minister of India, Indira Gandhi, daughter of the first prime minister, Jawaharlal Nehru. The strong-willed Iron Lady of India was in office for four consecutive terms until her assassination in 1984. Known for her formidable demeanour, Indira Gandhi let her guard down the moment Zerbanoo mentioned that her father Jawaharlal Nehru had once written a letter to her as a child. She responded, 'You must be a very special girl for my father to write a letter to you. Until now, I thought I was the only girl he ever wrote letters to.'

Indira admitted watching Zerbanoo's career with avidity as she took a special interest in British Indian politicians and saw her as a potential ambassador for India. Indira remarked that Indians abroad were often marginalized in their adoptive countries because they were not actively involved in public life.

They spoke about their second sons as having very different mindsets from their first-borns. Zerbanoo recounts the conversation she had during her tryst with one of the most powerful women in the history of the world: 'Indira spoke to me as a mother of two sons and not as the prime minister of the largest democracy of the world, which was endearing.'

Zerbanoo felt privileged when Indira Gandhi arranged to have a special pass for her to attend the CHOGM conference in Delhi. She remembers that special feeling as she walked behind Indira Gandhi into the opening session attended by all the leaders of the Commonwealth Countries.

As luck would have it, there was another opportunity the same evening to meet Indira Gandhi at an official reception hosted by the Queen of England at the British High Commission in Delhi. How the invitation to meet with the Queen came about, started with Zerbanoo being placed next to the widely-travelled industrialist, Sohrab Godrej, at a luncheon party hosted by a family friend.

They were making small talk when Sohrab Godrej casually asked her how he could make her trip to India more enjoyable. Not one to take a light-hearted dinner exchange seriously, she jokingly quipped, 'I would like to meet the Queen', forgetting all about it minutes later.

Within a couple of hours, the most extraordinary thing happened. Zerbanoo received an official invitation from the British High Commission to attend the party hosted by Queen Elizabeth for the Commonwealth Heads of Government.

Although all dressed up for the occasion, when Zerbanoo reached the British High Commission in Delhi (the venue of the reception), she was unusually apprehensive. She couldn't see Sohrab Godrej anywhere. Watching him walk in later had the British High Commissioner and the Maharaja of Baroda remark that the only person allowed to appear after the Queen's arrival was Sohrab Godrej.

Zerbanoo later wrote about her experience in a newspaper column titled, 'Meeting Two Queens in a Day: the Queen of England and Indira Gandhi, the Rani (Queen) of India.' A casual conversation over lunch had led to an invitation with the Queen and forged a lifelong friendship with Sohrab Godrej.

In his memoir titled *Abundant Living, Restless Striving* there is a touching account of Sohrab Godrej's final visit to London and how he collapsed in Zerbanoo's arms. It was as if their destinies were intricately tied together to the very end.

On a long-distance call, Sohrab informed Zerbanoo that he would travel to London to celebrate her fiftieth birthday. Whilst there, he was keen to visit the much talked about Millennium Dome. Zerbanoo was concerned about his health and insisted that he bring his private secretary, Rumi Majoo, along with him to London.

An extract in his memoir recounted by B.K. Karanjia reads:

Sohrab insisted on going to see the new Godrej office in London. Zerbanoo tried her best to dissuade him, but he insisted. To reach the office, he had to climb three flights of stairs, which he took in his stride. When he didn't return by 3.30 p.m., an anxious Zerbanoo rang up the office. Dorab

Mistry, who headed the Godrej Empire in Europe, told her that they wouldn't reach her till the evening, as Mr Godrej insisted on visiting the Millennium Dome too.

Zerbanoo started to worry about Sohrab Godrej because she knew that he had flown from India with a stopover in Paris and had driven straight from Heathrow Airport to her home in Harrow. He was jet-lagged but refused to rest. He had then driven to the Godrej office in London and was making his way to the Dome. It was too much for anyone even half his age.

The excerpt continues:

After the Millennium Dome, on the way to Zerbanoo's residence, the car got caught in a terrible traffic jam. According to the driver, Raj, Mr Godrej seemed to be in extreme discomfort, was lying back in his seat, totally exhausted, breathing heavily. Reaching Zerbanoo's house, Sohrab could hardly walk. So the driver and Majoo lifted him and carried him to a chair in the sitting room. He was breathless, couldn't utter a word; his nose was leaking, his hands cold as ice. A hot water bag was hastily brought. It didn't do much good. Majoo requested Zerbanoo to immediately send for a doctor. The ambulance arrived and they drove him to Northwick Park Hospital in seven or eight minutes. The Accident and Emergency Ward took him in. It was about eight o'clock in the evening. Zerbanoo accompanied them in the ambulance.

Unfortunately, within forty-eight hours Soli Godrej breathed his last. Zerbanoo called his nephews Adi and Jamshyd Godrej, who arrived before he died. On Sunday,

21 May 2000, his body was taken to the morgue. It was the day they were to have left for Paris for the ACTIM Conference.

Friend, confidante and mentor, it is difficult to label their unique relationship except that she sorely misses Sohrab Godrej's reassuring presence in her life. Zerbanoo often reminisces about the times he regaled her with stories of what India was like before Independence. His anecdotes always reflected his personal glimpses into the minds of powerful men and women he had interacted with in his lifetime. His off-the-cuff remarks were sprinkled with wry humour and great wisdom.

Recapturing the traumatic moments of wheeling Sohrab into the Accident and Emergency wing at Northwick Park Hospital, in Harrow, Zerbanoo smiles at the memory of the doctor on duty asking him when he had his last drink, to which he swiftly retorted he had given up drinking at the request of Mahatma Gandhi. He mumbled that probably the last time he had a drink was in Russia in the company of Stalin.

The doctor looked at me as if to say 'Who is this loony?' I had to tell him that the gentleman in front of him was one of India's most respected and influential industrialists. Also, the fact remains that he did know all the major players of the twentieth century and probably did drink vodka with Stalin. After that, he was immediately transferred to intensive care.

Recollecting poignant memories, she talks fondly about Sohrab's simple pleasures of life like cycling and travelling. Sohrab Godrej was a conservationist at heart with a deep interest in wildlife. A fascinating aspect of their relationship that stands out is that, in all the years he knew Zerbanoo, one of India's wealthiest men never gave her a gift.

However, he did host her son, Alexander's eighteenth birthday party while he was filming the iconic Bollywood film *Bombay Boys* in Mumbai. The occasion had the A-listers from the glamour industry assemble at the rooftop garden at Godrej Bhavan. The menu featured Zerbanoo's favourite dishes like ladyfingers and fried bananas served with other rich Parsi delicacies. On that special evening, Sohrab took Zerbanoo aside and confessed that although he was one of the most travelled men in the world, he didn't know what to give her. 'Therefore I have decided you must have the most wonderful thing in the world,' pulling out from his wallet a tattered Japanese postcard of a cherry tree in full bloom. Zerbanoo is yet to see a cherry tree in full bloom in Japan but she has planted a cherry orchard at the ASHA Centre. Now, every year, she is reminded of the most unusual and loving gift she ever received.

On yet another one of her trips to her motherland, this time to help set up the Charities Aid Foundation Bank in India, Zerbanoo was the personal guest of the Maharana of Udaipur at his palace – considered by Jackie Kennedy as the most beautiful place on earth. The Maharana treated Zerbanoo like one of the princesses of yore. When she had to fly to Delhi, he arranged for his private car to drive her from the palace onto the tarmac to step straight onto a small aircraft. Zerbanoo was already very queasy by the time she started to walk up the flight of stairs into the aircraft. The air-hostess looked equally nervous when Zerbanoo mentioned that she would like to take a front seat. The hostess explained that all the seats in the front row had already been taken by a minister who was travelling on the same flight.

The Indian minister, used to throwing his weight around, stubbornly refused to budge or move his bags off the seats, declaring, 'I am a VIP.'

Not one to be intimidated, Zerbanoo upstaged him: 'In that case, I am a VVIP.'

The minister was clearly annoyed by her defiant attitude. However, he underwent a rapid change of heart a few minutes later when he opened the complimentary copy of the *Times of India* newspaper and found a big picture of Zerbanoo staring back at him from the cover page. 'So you really are a VVIP,' he said sheepishly. After that, he was sweetness personified and went out of his way to be charming, allowing Zerbanoo to sit next to him in the front of the plane.

Back in England, Zerbanoo had enough fodder for her next column. She wrote: 'Politicians are here today and gone tomorrow. And who really is a VIP?'

Ironically, the minister lost the next elections and was history while Zerbanoo continues to collaborate with hundreds of people, working on solutions that initiate cultural shifts in polarized economies. She doesn't feel the need to label herself as anything.

Her independence and confidence give her the freedom to grow constantly and explore something new every day. In 1996, Zerbanoo was invited by the United States Information Agency's International Visitor Programme to visit America to promote mutual understanding through briefing sessions on defence and foreign policies. She was also privileged to be introduced to many of America's leading politicians and opinion-formers.

It was on that trip that she met His Excellency Jamsheed Marker in Washington. The veteran Pakistani diplomat is listed in the Guinness Book of World Records as having been an ambassador to more countries than any other person in the world.

He is a remarkable man. Dignified, courteous and the best diplomat I know. As I had fallen in love with America, a year later, Richard and I decided to take our boys to Disney World and explore America with them. Jamsheed and his beautiful wife Arnaz, President of All Pakistan Women's Association (APWA), allowed us to stay in their home in Florida. It was a dream holiday with the boys having the time of their lives jumping in and out of their pool and just causing havoc as boys do. Soon afterwards, Jamsheed came up to me and sweetly said, 'Would you mind if I returned to Washington DC? You know how welcome you are to stay here.'

He could have told me that we were driving him mad. We did enjoy Florida and then joined the Markers in their Washington home. It was an extraordinary arrival. It was a very hot day and the boys had decided to run wild in the Embassy garden under a water sprinkler to keep cool. I was reading when in walked Arnaz, pale and obviously shocked. President Haq had been assassinated on a plane and Pakistan was in a state of Emergency.

Some years later, Zerbanoo stayed with Arnaz and Jamsheed Marker again when he was the Chair of the United Nations

Security Council in New York and was privileged to see him in action. He commanded the respect of all the ambassadors there. His ease and intellectual brilliance were a study in understanding world dynamics as he helped bring about the resolution of the East Timor conflict and the independence of that nation.

Another vibrant personality who left a lasting impression on Zerbanoo in New York was Helen Gurley Brown, the editor-in-chief of *Cosmopolitan* and a pioneer for women in journalism, and named as one of the world's hundred most influential women that have ever lived. She was also the acclaimed author of *Sex and the Single Girl*, later made into a film starring Natalie Wood.

Helen was very pleased that Zerbanoo had been one of the British *Cosmopolitan* magazine's 'Women of Today' and invited her into her private domain. In her late seventies, Helen looked like a skinny schoolgirl, dressed in a short skirt. Sharing the secret of her success, Helen outlined the simple rules she had followed all her life: 'Write thank you letters and always tip the doorman. Most people forget to be nice to the man holding the door for them. Remember to be gracious and smile. Life is so strange that the doorman can land up as the president of the company.'

While there, Zerbanoo also attended the Television Awards Ceremony in Los Angeles. Sitting at the table reserved for the 'glitterati' of the long-running American TV soap opera *Dallas*, she sensed that Patrick Duffy, who played oil tycoon Bobby Ewing, and the other star cast present, were curious to find out who she was. Zerbanoo wasn't about to tell them that she had asked to be seated at their table so that she could have a picture of herself posing with Bobby to use in her forthcoming 1987 general election campaign in Britain. Zerbanoo smiled sweetly and with tongue-in-cheek said: 'I am the Princess of Zoroastria.'

Everyone felt good. She was even asked by American movie idol Robert Mitchum to have his photo shot with her. The picture still hangs in her younger brother Naswan's sitting room. Surprisingly, no one asked her where Zoroastria was. Zerbanoo assumed that geography was probably not their strong point. She remembers everyone that evening earnestly discussing the meaning of life and how important it was to have one's work recognized by others.

Zerbanoo ended the debate with, 'Life isn't rocket science. It begins and ends with acts of kindness. All you can take from life is what you have given away. She explained that in the Hindu scriptures it is put so poetically, 'We should be like a flower that gives of its perfume and honey but when the work is done it falls away quietly.'

Theatre director Adrian Locher adds, 'I can't see Zerbanoo falling away quietly! Her presence and vision will remain forever. For so many people there's life "before Zerbanoo" and life "after Zerbanoo". BZ and AZ.'

But the last word must go to the innocence of youth that always articulates the truth. When Zerbanoo's grandson, William Makepeace, was asked what he thought of his grandmother, he summed up everybody's feelings in one word, 'Supercalifragilisticexpialidocious.'

BEYOND THE BIOGRAPHY:
INNER THOUGHTS

It was an out-of-body experience.

Elevating, enriching, exhilarating, exhausting and all-consuming.

Writing a biography means putting your own life on hold.

For me, it involved taking up permanent residency in the crammed and creative mind of Zerbanoo Gifford. Settling into her crowded personal space, I attempted to explore her kaleidoscopic life, one dimension at a time.

Stepping into Zerbanoo's dizzyingly energetic, dramatic and frantic world was the most extraordinary experience that had me spinning at top speed into a heady vortex of raw emotions, inner thoughts and feelings. Every pore and fibre of my being was possessed by the powerful dynamics of an uncensored life.

My mind was in constant overdrive as I spent every waking hour thinking of the defining moments, milestones, mindset, characteristics, belief systems, values, incidents that best described my muse. For once, it was not all about me. A huge presence pervaded every ticking moment to grow into a magnificent obsession. My life took a complete backseat as I tried to understand the intricacies of a richly layered personal portrait that captured a section of history and vaulted over different worlds from the ancient to political, social, cultural, charitable, global and the esoteric.

Making thousands of notes in my diary alternated by keying in research on my laptop, recording sound bites, scribbling on scraps of paper, envelopes, napkins and anything in sight, I wasn't sure how I was going to eventually weave it all together.

A renowned biographer once compared writing life to sculpting with words. I think it is a lot more than that. Although I do agree that as one enthusiastically chisels away, the form that emerges slowly takes on a life of its own.

An Uncensored Life certainly found an expression infused with a magical life force as it manifested from a mountain of notes. Days ran into nights and months into two-and-a-half years, with the biography becoming such a huge part of my life that I was almost afraid to let go. A constant companion, it was my secret escape, a place I surreptitiously slipped into time and again. I found both comfort and solace in the parallel world in which I'd willingly lose myself.

I have yet to come across another human roller-coaster zooming at break-neck speed from one herculean project to another. Chronicling a remarkable life that has lived through extraordinary times and has been so widely written about, made it an even more daunting prospect. The challenge in working on a biographical portrait stems from exploring and acknowledging the changes and relationships that evolve during a lifetime, in a personal, professional, political, historial, social and spiritual context.

Everything I've been doing so far has been preparing me for

this very moment. I've long had the experience of probing the minds of stars and celebrities with a trail of transitory tinsel. Having been a journalist for the last three decades, I've been fortunate to closely connect with high achievers known for lofty thinking and far-reaching vision.

I started my career with being privy to the hedonistic lives of film stars, editing the popular *Stardust* magazine in India, which involved stepping into ivory towers to closely inspect the secret lives of superstars. The champagne evenings cotinued to flow into sequined nights with haute couture designers, models and photographers buzzing with creativity, glitz and glamour. Launching the largest-selling fashion glossy in the country, *Society Fashion* magazine, took me on a creative high like none other.

Moving cities further down the west coast of India, I took on the challenge of editing a newbie on the block, a city magazine aptly called *Citadel*, another magazine launched by the magazine magnate Nari Hira of Magna Publishing, in a city of fortresses. As *Citadel* took off and grew into the largest circulating city magazine in the country, I found a new perch on the Pune branch of the *Times of India*. Editing the Pune *Times of India*, from the stable of the largest circulated English daily newspaper in the world, was a challenging task. It also instilled in me the belief that we are all storytellers and that each one of us has a story to tell. It's through stories that inspire and empower that we reach out and connect with each other.

Flying to the other side of the world to the land of the long white cloud, New Zealand, I worked with the *Aucklander* magazine, and wrote for *The New Zealand Herald*. Over the years, I've enjoyed writing for several publishers in India,

New Zealand, the Middle East and South East Asia, as well as authoring the biography of Dr Grant, *The Making of a Legend*.

Currently, as news editor of the *Botany and Ormiston Times* in the City of Sails, I've had the opportunity to reach out to new communities and talk about their trials and triumphs.

Being a pen-pushing, passionate people-lover has had its share of silver linings. Most of all, it's given me a privileged entry to prod, search, question and soak in the personal mind space of larger-than-life demigods, glamorous matinee idols and eccentric mavericks. It has allowed me to closely examine the lives of international icons who radiate light and inspiration like metaphorical beacons. My journey so far has enabled me to understand the human psyche with all its complexities. It's fascinating to learn what makes some spirited individuals climb the slippery slope to the pinnacle of success as they stand tall and make a difference to the rest of humanity.

Blanking out of my life, as I willingly lived Zerbanoo's free-spirited one, was amply compensated with invaluable lessons that I gleaned from her life-scape. It was an open invitation to grab the gauntlet, take courage and have faith that there is justice for all. Everything we want is always on the other side of fear. Rising to the challenge without allowing pusillanimity to imprison us involves battling through the chaotic bylanes of life to achieve our true purpose.

Zerbanoo's life story is a source of self-discovery as it unveils a map of the many roads she travelled. It navigates through different cultural bridges while briefly stepping into the back alleys of violence and hate. Her story held a mirror to mine (like it will to yours). Its path meandered through the bylanes of Britain's colonial past that reeked of unremitting racial prejudice and gender discrimination that I must admit I have never experienced in my personal or professional life. The unfolding of Zerbanoo's life hits home a message that each one of us has the power to create the world we dream of. It is a powerful trigger, a timely reminder that we can fill up the unwritten pages of our lives with whatever story of greatness, moral sensibility or generosity we may want it to be.

The only thing that matters as you reach the last page of this uplifting testament of tenacity and ability to transform lives is what you take away from it, and how you use it to impact others. It could pique your curiosity, push you to take action, embrace a new challenge, ratchet the stakes to unthinkable levels of urgency or just make you stop and think – as it did me.

The book was conceived at a stage in my life when I asked the universe for an exhilarating challenge that would fill up my senses and consume me completely. I'm convinced there is a divine intervention of pure consciousness at work, here. It feels surreal as I look across at the stunning landscape that is halfway across the world. As I step into the sit-out of Zerbanoo's son Alex's apartment, which is surrounded with a tranquil view of the meadows, I'm reminded of the sheep back home leisurely nibbling away until the cows come home. The scenario is a fine study in contradictions. The laid-back ambience is in sharp contrast to Zerbanoo's 'let's do it right now' disposition that drives her, and everyone around her, sprinting into action. She energetically sets a fast-forward tempo and sparks electricity that lights up the entire ASHA Centre.

To give you a glimpse of Zerbanoo's fierce sense of urgency, I recall the time the two of us were driving back from London to Gloucestershire. As the car gathered momentum on the express lane, I casually mentioned to Zerbanoo that being a Rotarian with the Rotary Club of Somerville, in Auckland, New Zealand, I was keen to attend a Rotary meeting in England some day. 'Some day' is a phrase that obviously doesn't exist in her lexicon. The very next moment, she swerved the car, taking an immediate exit to the village of Hungerford. Suddenly, we were off the motorway whilst I sat open-mouthed with words hanging midsentence.

Even before I could comprehend what had just happened, she was introducing me to the owner of an antique shop, Annabel King. Annabel, I discovered, was president next of the Rotary Club of Hungerford. Being an old friend and loyal client of Annabel's, Zerbanoo did not waste a second connecting me with a fellow Rotarian. We attended their Rotary meeting the very next week. Zerbanoo was invited to be the guest speaker. In a blink of an eye, she had added momentum to the entire sequence of events which, left up to me, would have taken a while to transpire. And it didn't end there. The Rotary Club of Hungerford was invited to the beautifully landscaped ASHA Centre in Gloucestershire, which they visited two months later.

My daughter Sanaya, who joined me at Alex's apartment for a weekend, still laughs at my feeble attempts to harness the 'power of now'. It was like being on roller-skates. I often found myself running up the flight of stairs that connects to Zerbanoo's home with uncombed hair, trying to button my shirt, slip on my shoes and grab my coat, diary, scarf and laptop – all at once. It was an elementary lesson that it is not only time and tide, but even Zerbanoo, waits for no man (not even her biographer). She often reminds me of a quivering arrow, intoxicated with a burst of energy and passion for life. With so much to do and so little time, she is always on the run, fired up with new ideas, theories and an exhaustive list of things to do. Space shuttle Zerbanoo, did someone say?

Apart from trailing her, playing armchair psychoanalyst and spending endless hours talking to her friends, family, colleagues and the people whose lives she has touched, I also braved it out in the cold attic at her home. Leafing through thousands of press cuttings, personal letters, cards and other memorabilia, soaking in every aspect of her eventful life was a sepia-toned journey, an insightful flashback into her past.

Suddenly, my laptop became my most precious possession in the world. Most of all, working on the biography was awe-inspiring. I couldn't quite fathom how the universal spirit scripts the intricate wisdom of billions of lives whilst I grappled with just the one.

It's challenging to create shards of meaning whilst getting under the skin of the subject and also recording the many said and unsaid words.

There were uncomfortable moments when I unwittingly uncovered old wounds that still festered beneath superficial scars. I had to stop myself from wanting to hug Zerbanoo and rock her in my arms for making her delve deep into past hurts and misgivings that were best forgotten. It felt like drawing blood from old memories that have been safely buried in the recesses of one's mind. Those were dark places that left her feeling vulnerable and exposed. And yet, she bravely agreed to open doors that had been locked up and the keys thrown away. It was a catharsis of sorts as her bitter-sweet memories gushed out.

While practically every chapter of the biography resonates

with a triumph of hope, justice and a grand vision, putting them in order was an uphill task. Part of it could be attributed to the fact that Zerbanoo does not have the patience for speaking in sequence. Living in the times when politicians are made accountable and being verbally flogged for transgressions (however minor) in their shameful past, it was difficult to stop Zerbanoo from taking off tangentially.

She was trenchant about the issues that made sordid headlines in the British media. We would often spend hours discussing political scandals being finally exposed. For Zerbanoo, it was payback time as she clearly identified with the horrors of living with misogynistic threats, racial prejudice and the plain apathy of self-serving individuals who masqueraded as political leaders. The public humiliation of former politicians and celebrities found guilty of indecent assault on minors proved there was justice at last. It was proof that the truth does ultimately prevail even if it has been swept under the carpet for decades.

An Uncensored Life contextualizes a life that provides a bridge between then and now. The biography traces the life of a housewife, and mother of two, with the resourcefulness to rise above the yoke of conformity. Unconventional in thought, she spontaneously broke rules, took chances and traversed a different landscape without faltering despite the rocky mountain terrains. It reiterates that you don't have to be rich, powerful or a nerd to make a world of difference. As long as you have purity of heart and intention, there will be synchronicity that will explore the strength and creativity that you never knew existed within you.

Admittedly, when I started writing this biography, I was metaphorically standing at the source of the river, contemplating and wondering which path it would eventually take to reach its confluence. But now, as I key in the last few words, my heart tells me that this is the precise moment where the river meets the ocean. It takes with it, in its tide, stories of hope, fearlessness and fortitude that will touch and illuminate lives on different shores.

ACKNOWLEDGEMENTS

I am grateful to Zerbanoo for welcoming me into her home and filling my life with warmth, laughter and a crazy buzz. Also, for allowing me to step into the sacred space and trusting me even when my probing questions made her feel vulnerable. I cannot thank you enough for having documented and meticulously archived all your letters, press cuttings, cards, photographs and other memorabilia that helped plug the holes when time-bound memories occasionally lapsed.

A special thank you to Richard for all those warm and delicious salmon and veggie meals that appeared magically when Zerbanoo and I were lost in discussion and continued talking without pause. Also, for allowing me to hog all of Zerbanoo's attention for those months I spent doing research.

A big hug to Alex for so graciously allowing me to stay in his fabulous flat that is surrounded by divinity and overlooks the most spectacular landscape. I couldn't have asked for a better setting to start working on a life portrait.

To Mark for giving me the first cue on the path the book should follow. And to Adrian for all his valuable inputs and for always being there to fall back on.

This book would not have seen the light of the day had it not been for Stevie and his back-office support. There is a very good reason why Zerbanoo has nicknamed him 'Stevie Wonder'. Thank you for always finding the right version of the chapter from the ninety-nine others.

Sandy, Lucie, Khalid, Madelina and all the volunteers who make ASHA a happy place – thank you for instantly embracing me into your fold.

To little Makepeace for adding a special sparkle to a fascinating biographical journey of a thousand miles.

To my daughter Sanaya for encouraging me and being a rock when I wondered if I could do justice to the biography. Thank you for all your helpful suggestions and your brilliant feedback that helped me shape and polish the book. Also, to my husband Khushroo for being so understanding, patient and for allowing me to follow my heart – even if it meant stretching a two-month holiday into nine-month working holiday away from home.

How can I forget my biggest cheerleaders, my late mum Freny and my grandmother Dhunmai, who eagerly checked on the progress of the book. They may not be here in person, but are certainly present in spirit.

This HarperCollins production could not have come to life without the astute book-doctors, Consulting Editor Sathya Saran and Commissioning Editor Debasri Rakshit. Ladies, please take a bow for making it all happen!

To Supriya Mahajan for the beautiful design and to the rest of the HarperCollins team who silently work behind the scenes.

My gratitude list is incomplete without Bachi Karkaria, director, Times Literary Festival India. I am thankful for your unstinted support and to the Times Group in New Zealand for